TRANSFORMED BY GOD

NEW COVENANT LIFE AND MINISTRY

David G. Peterson

IVP Academic

An imprint of InterVarsity Press
Downers Grove, Illinois

InterVarsity Press
P.O. Box 1400, Downers Grove, IL 60515-1426
Internet: www.ivpress.com
E-mail: email@ivpress.com

Published in the United States of America by InterVarsity Press, Downers Grove, Illinois, with permission from Inter-Varsity Press, England.

InterVarsity Press® is the book-publishing division of InterVarsity Christian Fellowship/USA®, a movement of students and faculty active on campus at hundreds of universities, colleges and schools of nursing in the United States of America, and a member movement of the International Fellowship of Evangelical Students. For information about local and regional activities, write Public Relations Dept., InterVarsity Christian Fellowship/USA, 6400 Schroeder Rd., P.O. Box 7895, Madison, WI 53707-7895, or visit the IVCF website at <www.intervarsity.org>.

While all stories in this book are true, some names and identifying information in this book have been changed to protect the privacy of the individuals involved.

Cover design: Cindy Kiple
Cover image: © Giorgio Magini/iStockphoto

ISBN 978-0-8308-3977-3

Printed in the United States of America ∞

Library of Congress Cataloging-in-Publication Data

Peterson, David, 1944-
  Transformed by God : new covenant life and ministry / David G. Peterson.
    p. cm.
  Includes bibliographical references and index.
  ISBN 978-0-8308-3977-3 (pbk. : alk. paper)
  1. Covenants—Biblical teaching. 2. Bible. O.T. Jeremiah XXXI, 31-34—Theology. 3. Bible. N.T.—Theology 4. Bible. O.T. Jeremiah—Relation to the N.T. 5. Bible. N.T.—Relation to Jeremiah. 6. Christian life—Biblical teaching. I. Title.
  BS1525.6.C6P48 2012
  231.7'6—dc23

2012009665

P	18	17	16	15	14	13	12	11	10	9	8	7	6	5	4	3	2	1
Y	27	26	25	24	23	22	21	20	19	18	17	16	15	14	13	12		

I dedicate this book to my grandchildren,
Emma, Sam and Charlie, with a prayer that they might
come to experience and enjoy for themselves the
great blessings won for us by the Lord Jesus Christ,
when he established the New Covenant.

CONTENTS

ABBREVIATIONS

1QS   Dead Sea Scrolls, *Rule of the Community* from Qumran cave 1

11QMelch.   Dead Sea Scrolls, *Melchizedek* text from Qumran cave 11

AB   Anchor Bible

AnBib   Analecta biblica

ASV   American Standard Version

AV   Authorized Version (King James Version)

BDAG   W. Bauer, W. F. Arndt, F. W. Gingrich and F. W. Danker, *A Greek-English Lexicon of the New Testament and Other Early Christian Literature*, 3rd ed. (Chicago: University of Chicago Press, 1999)

BDB   *A Hebrew and English Lexicon of the Old Testament*, ed. F. Brown, S. R. Driver and C. A. Briggs (Oxford: Clarendon, 1977)

BECNT   Baker Exegetical Commentary on the New Testament

BNTC   Black's New Testament Commentaries

CBQ   *Catholic Biblical Quarterly*

EDNT   *Exegetical Dictionary of the New Testament*, ed. H. Balz and G. Schneider, 3 vols. (ET Grand Rapids: Eerdmans, 1990–3)

EvQ   *Evangelical Quarterly*

ESV   English Standard Version

ET   English translation

ExpT *Expository Times*

ICC International Critical Commentary

JBL *Journal of Biblical Literature*

JBLMS Journal of Biblical Literature Monograph Series

JETS *Journal of the Evangelical Theological Society*

JSNT *Journal for the Study of the New Testament*

JSNTSS Journal for the Study of the New Testament
Supplement Series

JSOTSS Journal for the Study of the Old Testament
Supplement Series

JTS *Journal of Theological Studies*

LumVie *Lumière et vie*

LXX Septuagint (Greek Version of the Old Testament)

NASB New American Standard Bible

Neot *Neotestamentica*

NIB *The New Interpreter's Bible*, ed. L. E. Keck, 12 vols.
(Nashville: Abingdon, 1993–2002)

NICNT New International Commentary on the New
Testament

NICOT New International Commentary on the Old
Testament

NIDNTT *New International Dictionary of New Testament Theology*,
ed. C. Brown, 3 vols. (Exeter: Paternoster, 1975,
1976, 1978)

NIDOTTE *New International Dictionary of Old Testament Theology
and Exegesis*, ed. W. A. VanGemeren, 5 vols. (Grand
Rapids: Zondervan; Carlisle: Paternoster, 1997)

NIGTC New International Greek Testament Commentary

NIV New International Version

NIVAC New International Version Application Commentary

NKJV New King James Version

NRSV New Revised Standard Version

NSBT New Studies in Biblical Theology

NT New Testament

OT Old Testament

par. parallel
PNTC The Pillar New Testament Commentary
RevB *Revue Biblique*
SBL Studies in Biblical Literature
SC Sources chrétiennes (Paris: Cerf, 1943–)
SJT *Scottish Journal of Theology*
SNTSMS Society for New Testament Studies Monograph Series
SP Sacra pagina
TDNT *Theological Dictionary of the New Testament*, ed. G. Kittel and G. Friedrich; tr. G. W. Bromiley, 10 vols. (Grand Rapids: Eerdmans, 1964–76)
TDOT *Theological Dictionary of the Old Testament*, ed. G. J. Botterweck and H. Ringgren; tr. J. T. Willis, G. W. Bromiley and D. E. Green, 14 vols. (Grand Rapids: Eerdmans, 1964–76)
TNIV Today's New International Version
tr. translated by/translation
TynB *Tyndale Bulletin*
WBC Word Biblical Commentary
WUNT Wissenschaftliche Untersuchungen zum Neuen Testament

INTRODUCTION

Across the centuries, as people have considered their individual and social needs, many solutions for transforming human existence have been offered – psychological, political and religious. But the New Testament claims that genuine and lasting change can be found only in Jesus Christ. The transformation he makes possible is *spiritual*, establishing an eternal relationship with God for us, *moral*, enabling a new life of obedience and service, and *physical*, bringing us ultimately to share in his resurrection from death in a new creation. Foundational to this teaching in several New Testament writings is Jeremiah's promise of 'a new covenant' (Jer. 31:31–34).

This passage climaxes a series of oracles about the restoration of the relationship between God and his people after the Babylonian exile in the sixth century BC. It picks up a number of themes highlighted in previous chapters and further developed in subsequent chapters. In several important ways it encapsulates Jeremiah's hopes for the future. There are parallel predictions in other prophetic books, but Jeremiah 31:31–34 appears to have been particularly influential for New Testament writers. Indeed, what we call 'the New

Testament' is effectively a collection of texts explaining how the New Covenant has been established and what it means for Christians.[1]

Direct reference is made to the promised New Covenant in Luke 22:20, 1 Corinthians 11:25, 2 Corinthians 3:6, and Hebrews 8:8–12; 10:15–17.[2] Paul's argument in 2 Corinthians 3 also draws on Ezekiel's prophecies, to explain how the Holy Spirit is instrumental in the promised renewal. In other contexts, the apostle alludes to particular New Covenant promises, either from Jeremiah or parallel prophecies, sometimes conflating these texts (e.g. Rom. 2:15; 5:5; 6:17; 10:9–10; 11:26–27; Gal. 4:24–31; 1 Thess. 4:9). The Johannine writings proclaim a new knowledge of God that is consistent with Jeremiah's predictions.

When New Testament writers quote words or phrases from Jeremiah's oracle, it is often clear from the context that the contents and logic of Jeremiah 31:31–34 have significantly influenced the way they think about transformation in Christ. The definitive forgiveness of sins achieved by his sacrificial death brings a new knowledge or experience of God and his grace, which transforms hearts and minds, leading to a new devotion to God and obedience to his will. In this way, the people of the New Covenant are established in an eternal relationship with God. Luke-Acts in particular shows how transformed Israelites form the basis of a renewed community that embraces every nation.[3]

---

1. The word 'testament' derives from the Latin *testamentum*, which was used to translate Hebrew *bĕrît* and Greek *diathēkē* (covenant). By the beginning of the third century AD, the title 'the New Testament' is used for the Gospels and other Christian writings, recognized together with 'the Old Testament' as Scripture. Cf. S. Lehne, *The New Covenant in Hebrews*, JSNTSS 44 (Sheffield: Sheffield Academic, 1990), pp. 88–89.

2. The New Covenant is also mentioned by name in Heb. 9:15, 12:24, and called 'a better covenant' in 7:22, 8:6, and 'the eternal covenant' in 13:20.

3. Luke shows the need for the Messiah to inaugurate the New Covenant by his death and pour out the promised Holy Spirit. Acts presents the fulfilment of these events as the basis for calling Israelites to respond and become the source of New Covenant blessing to the nations.

New Covenant theology is central to New Testament thinking about the saving work of Christ and the way it is appropriated by believers. It has profound implications for Christian ministry, with respect to both evangelism and the nurture of believers. It is the basis of much teaching about perseverance, growth and change. It is a key for understanding the differences between pre-Christ and post-Christ experiences of God. In terms of the Bible's teaching as a whole, it shows how the Christian dispensation is a fulfilment and perfection of the covenant first established by God with Abraham and his offspring.

The first four chapters of this book formed the basis for a series of lectures given in May 2011 at the Oak Hill College Annual School of Theology in London. I am grateful to the Principal, the Reverend Dr Michael Ovey, for inviting me back and giving me the opportunity to speak on a topic that has occupied my mind for some time. It was a great delight to meet former colleagues and students and to be stimulated by their questions and comments to develop the work into its present form.

Biblical theology must have a pastoral application, because God reveals his character and will to bring us into relationship with himself, not simply to stimulate our thinking. He nurtures and sustains us in that relationship by his self-revelation, and ultimately brings us to share in his glory through his word and his Spirit. So, although there is some engagement with academic issues in this book, the main aim is to expose the way New Testament writers understand and apply New Covenant expectations to Christian life and ministry.

1. THE NEW COVENANT IN JEREMIAH

Jeremiah's promise of 'a new covenant' can be found in his 'Book of Comfort' (30 – 31). This is a collection of oracles, mostly poetical in form, offering hope to Israel and Judah in the seventh and sixth centuries BC.[1] In earlier chapters the theme of judgment predominates, but there are also important anticipations of the hopeful messages found in chapters 30 – 31. Similar promises are reiterated and expanded in later chapters, in the prose section that follows (32 – 33), and even in Jeremiah's oracles against the nations (46 – 51). So the broader context fills out the meaning of the specific set of promises in the prophecy of the New Covenant in 31:31–34.

---

1. Although the northern kingdom had been in exile since 722 BC, a century or more later, Jeremiah called upon faithless Israel to return to the Lord (3:11–14) and promised that the restored nation would contain representatives from both the exiled northern and southern kingdoms (e.g. 3:18; 30:3–4; 31:23–40).

Jeremiah's calling

Jeremiah testifies that the Lord appointed him to be 'a prophet to
the nations' (1:5). This surprising designation is reinforced by a
divine promise, 'I have set you this day over nations and over
kingdoms' (1:10). Here the prophet is given a twofold task. Negatively,
through the proclamation of the words God puts in his mouth (1:9),
he is 'to pluck up and to break down, to destroy and to overthrow'.
Although his call is to the nations, his first commission (1:11–19) is
directed towards Jerusalem. In effect, he will 'dismantle and destroy
all that constitutes the Jerusalem establishment'.[2] As his prophetic
ministry unfolds, it becomes clear that this takes place through the
Babylonian invasion in the sixth century BC and its aftermath.
Positively, however, Jeremiah is used 'to build and to plant': to restore
the devastated people of God and to open the way for survivors
from the nations to share their blessings (3:16–17; 12:14–17; 16:19–
21). Judah is merely one of the nations (cf. 9:26), yet her promised
redemption affords hope to the whole world.

The divine work of plucking up and tearing down is mentioned
together with that of building and planting several times in the book
of Jeremiah (12:14–17; 18:7–9; 24:6; 31:28, 40; 42:10; 45:4). God's
commissioning of the prophet in 1:10 relates to the great things
God will accomplish through the faithful proclamation of his *words*.
Attached to this commission is the promise of God 'I am watching
over my word to perform it' (1:12). So,

> Jeremiah's vocation is not simply to talk about, describe, report, or
> anticipate destruction and restoration but to enact all that by his
> utterance. Prophetic utterance is presented here as *performative*: the
> prophetic utterance performs what it says.[3]

---

2. W. Brueggemann, *The Theology of the Book of Jeremiah* (Cambridge:
   Cambridge University Press, 2007), p. 60.
3. Ibid., p. 61 (original emphasis).

The broken covenant

The first main section of the book records many indictments of the nation's rebellion against God (2 – 25). From the start, Judah's culpability is shown to be greater than Israel's (2:1 – 6:30). Even when the northern kingdom was 'sent away' because of all her 'adulteries' in the eighth century BC, the southern kingdom of Judah did not return to the Lord with all her heart, but only 'in pretence' (3:6–10).

Judgment for rebellion

As the prophet proceeds to unveil Judah's idolatry, he predicts the destruction of the Jerusalem temple (7:1 – 10:25). He continues to dismantle Judah's 'symbolic universe' by insisting that their covenant status cannot save them from the judgment of exile (11:1 – 17:27).[4] Judah has forfeited her privileged 'insider' status and must face the fate once reserved for the nations (18:1 – 20:18). The failure of the Davidic kings to lead the people in God's way means that judgment must fall here too (21:1 – 24:10). 'Nothing can save Judah: neither temple, covenant, its status as an elect people, nor Davidic king.'[5]

Jeremiah's rhetoric of judgment 'is a vehicle by which the fierce sovereignty of YHWH, in the face of challenge, is vigorously reasserted over a recalcitrant covenant partner'.[6] In the prophet's eyes, their idolatry was the ultimate betrayal of the relationship God had established with them. This is often portrayed in terms of spiritual adultery. However, Israel's unfaithfulness to God also found expression in injustice (5:1–6, 26–31), greed (6:13–15), hypocritical worship (7:1–26), deceit and oppression (9:2–16), and failing to honour the sabbath (17:19–27). Jeremiah condemns prophets, priests and kings

---

4. Cf. L. Stulman, 'The Prose Sermons as Hermeneutical Guide to Jeremiah 1–25: The Deconstruction of Judah's Symbolic World', in A. R. P. Diamond, K. M. O'Connor and L. Stulman (eds.), *Troubling Jeremiah*, JSOTSS 260 (Sheffield: Sheffield Academic Press, 1999), pp. 34–63.
5. Ibid., p. 60.
6. Brueggemann, *Theology*, p. 77.

for encouraging such resistance to God and his will (2:8; 5:12–13, 30–31; 6:13–15; 22:1–30; 23:9–40).

Uncircumcised hearts

The word 'covenant' occurs some twenty-three times in this book, mostly with reference to the covenant made by God with his people at Sinai, when he brought them out of Egypt (11:4). The Hebrew term *běrît* means 'imposition', 'liability' or 'obligation'.[7] In the book of Jeremiah there are many allusions to the exodus experience, to the law and commandments of God, and to the consequences of obedience or disobedience. Loyalty to God and sincere acceptance of the obligations of his covenant belong together in the teaching of this prophet.

The broken covenant is the central theme in 11:1–17, where the curses outlined in Deuteronomy 27 – 30 are shown to be already in operation. This prose section introduces a collection of oracles (11:1 – 17:25) developing the argument. The foundational promise of the Sinai covenant was that if they listened to God's voice and did what he commanded, he would be with them to bless them as his own special people (Exod. 19:5–6). However, echoing once more the language of Deuteronomy, the prophet claims that they 'did not obey or incline their ear, but everyone walked in the stubbornness of his evil heart' (11:8; cf. 17:9–10).

As a nation, therefore, they needed to be circumcised to the Lord in their hearts (4:1–4; cf. 9:25–26; Deut. 10:16). This teaching indicates that 'the physical rite of circumcision could never realize the purpose of the covenant if the heart remained foreign to it'.[8]

---

7. M. Weinfeld, *TDOT* 2:255. The word *běrît* is used in Scripture to describe binding commitments between human beings or between God and human beings. Cf. P. R. Williamson, *Sealed with an Oath: Covenant in God's Unfolding Purpose*, NSBT 23 (Downers Grove: InterVarsity Press; Nottingham: Apollos, 2007), pp. 36–43.

8. J. A. Thompson, *The Book of Jeremiah*, NICOT (Grand Rapids: Eerdmans, 1980), p. 216. Circumcision was meant to be an expression of surrender to the will of God in every area of life. As in Deuteronomy, the diagnosis of Israel's condition is couched by Jeremiah in terms that anticipate the cure (Jer. 24:7; 31:33; 32:39–40).

Whatever was hindering their receptivity to the word of God needed to be removed. But, as Moses predicted, only God could accomplish this, when he restored his people after the punishment of exile (Deut. 30:6).

As elsewhere in Scripture, the heart is 'the primary locus of divine evaluation of a people's spiritual state'.[9] The heart refers to the totality of one's inner life, including the intellect, the will and the emotions. Jeremiah indicates that the stubbornness of the human heart is the fundamental cause of every form of idolatry and disobedience to God's commands (7:24; 17:1–2, 5, 9–10). In line with the warning of Deuteronomy 28, the prophet goes on to proclaim that the Lord will deliberately abandon Judah and Jerusalem to a disaster from which they cannot escape (11:11–13; cf. 13:1–27). So irrevocable is this punishment that Jeremiah is told not to pray for his people any more (11:14; cf. 7:16; 14:11–12; 15:1–2).

Messages of hope

Mercy
Although the overwhelming emphasis is on judgment in the early chapters of this book, there are intimations of hope. For example, Jeremiah is told to call the former northern kingdom of Israel, deported by the Assyrians in 721 BC, to return to the Lord. God graciously promises them

> I will not look on you in anger,
> > for I am merciful.
> (3:12)[10]

---

9. A. Luc, *NIDOTTE* 2:751.
10. These words addressed 'towards the north' (3:12) are to 'faithless Israel'. The oracle is paralleled in 31:2–6, 15–22, where the prophet uses 'Ephraim' as a parallel term for the northern kingdom. Jeremiah's hope for a reunification of Judah and the northern kingdom is proclaimed in 3:12–15. Cf. Thompson, *Jeremiah*, pp. 199, 566.

But Israel is required to acknowledge her guilt and rebellion, expressed in scattering her 'favours' on foreign gods and not obeying the voice of God (3:13). Obedience was clearly a fundamental requirement for the covenant people (7:22–26; Exod. 19:5; Deut. 28:1–2).[11]

The challenge to repent is repeated with the assurance

> for I am your master;
>> I will take you, one from a city and two from a family,
> and I will bring you to Zion.
>
> (3:14)

A process of election within Israel is signalled here, as in the remnant theology of 23:3; 31:7. Bringing them to Zion suggests that representatives of the various tribes would be reunited at a single sanctuary once more. This reunion is made explicit in 3:18, at the climax of a passage anticipating the promises of the New Covenant.[12]

Later, in his letter to the Judean exiles in Babylon, Jeremiah indicates God's intention to visit them and fulfil his promise to bring them back to their land (29:10–14). His mercy is expressed in terms of 'plans for wholeness and not for evil, to give you a future and a hope' (v. 11). Since the broken covenant is linked with worshipping and serving other gods (22:9), the Lord's saving initiative will enable his restored people to call upon him and pray to him again, with the assurance that he will hear them (29:12).

The book culminates with a series of judgments against the nations (46 – 52), climaxing with a prediction of the utter destruction

---

11. However, Brueggemann, *Theology*, pp. 118–119, misses the point that God's offer of mercy and restoration appears to be the motivation for repentance and obedience in passages such as 3:12–14; 12:15–17.

12. Earlier prophets had spoken about the reunification of northern and southern kingdoms (e.g. Hos. 3:5; Mic. 2:12), but here the reunification takes place only after both groups have undergone exile (cf. Ezek. 37:15–28; Isa. 11:10–16).

of Babylon. In this context, the hope of restoration is once more articulated (50:4–5, 19–20, 28; 51:36–37, 45–46).[13] In that time,

> the people of Israel and the people of Judah shall come together, weeping as they come, and they shall seek the LORD their God. They shall ask the way to Zion, with faces turned towards it, saying, 'Come, let us join ourselves to the LORD in an everlasting covenant that will never be forgotten.' (50:4–5; cf. 31:8–9)

Moreover, God promises that in those days and at that time, 'iniquity shall be sought in Israel, and there shall be none, and sin in Judah, and none shall be found, for I will pardon those whom I leave as a remnant' (50:20; cf. 31:7).

Knowledge and understanding

The comprehensiveness of this restoration is indicated by God's promise to give his people shepherds after his own heart, who will feed them 'with knowledge and understanding' (3:15). This is related to the problem of unfaithful rulers, who have led the people astray (23:1–4; cf. Ezek. 34:1–22). In this connection, a specific promise is given about God delivering his people through the righteous offspring of David, the king he would raise up to 'execute justice and righteousness in the land' (23:5–6; 30:9; 33:14–17; cf. Isa. 11:1–9; Ezek. 34:23–24; 37:24–25).

Such knowledge and understanding would bring God's faithless children to acknowledge that they no longer needed the ark of the covenant (3:16). The ark represented God's ruling presence amongst his people (Lev. 16:2, 13; 2 Kgs 19:15; Ps. 80:1), and it contained the deeds of the covenant established through Moses. But the time would come when this symbolism would give way to the reality to which it pointed. Jerusalem itself would be called 'the throne of the Lord', and all nations would gather to it, 'to the presence of the

---

13. K. T. Aitken, 'The Oracles Against Babylon in Jeremiah 50–51: Structures and Perspectives', *TynB* 35 (1984), pp. 31–36, observes that Jer. 50 is as much about hope for Judah as it is about judgment for Babylon.

LORD in Jerusalem' (3:17; cf. Ezek. 37:26–28; 48:35; Isa. 2:2–3). This transformation of worship, involving people from every nation, would take place because the nations would no more 'stubbornly follow their own evil heart'.

A new heart

Israel was like the nations in having a 'heart' problem, which could be cured only by divine action (4:4; 9:25–26; 11:8; 18:12). A process of election and transformation would begin within Israel and extend to the nations. God's intention to 'plant' the returning exiles in the land he gave to their forefathers and 'not uproot them' is associated with the promise to 'give them a heart to know that I am the LORD' (24:6–7). A changed 'heart' would result in the re-establishment of the covenant relationship on a permanent basis: 'they shall be my people and I will be their God, for they shall return to me with their whole heart' (24:7). This promise is central to the New Covenant oracle in 31:33.

The same promise is restated in 32:38–41, where God undertakes to give them 'one heart and one way, that they may fear me for ever, for their own good and the good of their children after them'. Here God also undertakes to make with them 'an everlasting covenant, that I will not turn away from doing good to them'.[14] For their part, the assurance is given that 'I will put the fear of me in their hearts, that they may not turn from me', and the extraordinary claim is made that 'I will rejoice in doing them good, and I will plant them in this land in faithfulness, with all my heart and all my soul.' God's faithfulness and love are expressed here in a commitment of heart and soul to the relationship he has established with his people (cf. 31:20). His gracious initiative will make possible a change of their attitude and commitment.

---

14. The expression 'everlasting covenant' (*běrît 'ôlām*) is used with reference to God's covenant with Noah and every living creature (Gen. 9:16), his covenant with Israel (Exod. 31:16; Lev. 24:8; 1 Chr. 16:17; Ps. 105:10; Isa. 24:5), his covenant with David (2 Sam. 23:5), and the New Covenant (Isa. 55:3; Jer. 32:40; 50:5; Ezek. 16:60; 37:26).

Nations blessed

Despite Jeremiah's focus on God's special choice and purpose for Israel, there are remarkable hints of his intention to bless the nations together with Israel. So in 12:14–17 there is a warning of destruction given to nations who 'touch the heritage that I have given my people Israel to inherit'. Yet there is also the promise of compassion and hope for these nations: 'if they will diligently learn the ways of my people, to swear by my name, "As the LORD lives," even as they taught my people to swear by Baal, then they shall be built up in the midst of my people' (cf. 3:16–17).

Again in 16:19–21, following a promise of Israel's restoration (16:14–15), there is a prediction that the nations will come from the ends of the earth to Israel's God, confessing the lie of idolatry and the power and might of the Lord. With such predictions, we may hear an echo of the foundational promise to Abram to make his offspring a blessing to the nations: 'I will bless those who bless you, and him who dishonours you I will curse, and in you all the families of the earth shall be blessed' (Gen. 12:3; cf. Gen. 18:18; 22:18; 26:4–5; Jer. 4:1–2).

The Book of Comfort

Jeremiah 30 – 31 gathers together and repeats various messages of hope found in the preceding chapters. The prophet is summoned by God to 'write in a book all the words that I have spoken to you' (30:2).[15] God is about to restore the fortunes of his people, and bring Israel and Judah back to the land he gave them, to take possession

---

15. The word translated 'book' (*sēper*) can refer to a document of any kind (cf. 36:2, 4, *měgillat-sēper* [scroll-book]). J. R. Lundbom, *Jeremiah 21–36*, AB (New York: Doubleday, 2004), pp. 368–369, views Jer. 30 – 31 as the original 'Book of Comfort', and suggests that chapters 32–33 were added later to form a larger 'Book of Restoration'. 'Restore the/their fortunes' forms an inclusion between 30:3 and 33:26, and this key expression is also found in 31:23; 32:44; 33:7, 11.

of it (30:3–4). Following this brief introduction, a series of oracles give a fuller picture of what will happen when God acts. Restoration is the main theme, and this involves the re-establishment of God's people, the rebuilding of Jerusalem, and the inauguration of a new covenant.

Comprehensive restoration

A time of great distress is coming for Jacob, 'yet he shall be saved out of it' (30:7). God will release his people from captivity 'and foreigners shall no more make a servant of him' (30:8). The positive outcome will be their willingness to 'serve the LORD their God and David their king', whom God will raise up for them (30:9). Some transformation of heart is implied by this willingness to serve. The Davidic king will be the agent of God's perfect rule (cf. 23:5–6; 33:14–17; cf. Isa. 11:1–9; Ezek. 34:23–24; 37:24–25).

In the time of judgment that is coming upon the nations, the Lord will not make 'a full end' of Israel, but will discipline his people 'in just measure' (30:11; cf. 4:27; 5:10, 18; 46:28). The punishment of Israel will be great, because her guilt is great and her sins are flagrant (30:12–15), but God will devour her enemies and restore his people to full health (30:16–17). Restoration is portrayed in material and spiritual terms: dwellings and cities will be rebuilt, and

> out of them shall come songs of thanksgiving,
>   and the voices of those who celebrate.
> (30:18–19)

Covenantal restoration

The covenantal dimensions of this restoration are clearly set forth in 30:19–21. God will multiply his people and make them honoured. He will re-establish their community by punishing their oppressors and enabling a ruler to come from their midst to lead the nation in the ways of God. The Lord declares once more, 'you shall be my people, and I will be your God' (cf. 7:23; 11:4; 31:33; Exod. 6:7; 19:5; Lev. 26:12; Deut. 29:13; Ezek. 36:28). Even in the midst of judgment, the Lord will be 'the God of all the clans of Israel', and insists that 'they shall be my people' (30:23 – 31:1).

Israel's captivity and restoration is linked with the exodus deliverance under Moses (31:2–3). Two significant covenant terms are used to describe the way God first revealed himself to Israel and subsequently remained committed to the welfare of his people. The Lord says,

> I have loved you with an everlasting love;
> therefore I have continued my faithfulness to you.

So the promise to rebuild them is based on his love and faithfulness, as expressed in the history of his relationship with them. That restoration is once more portrayed in both material and spiritual terms (31:3–6).

The new exodus theme continues in 31:7–14. God will bring his people 'from the north country' and gather them 'from the farthest parts of the earth'. On the journey he will supply all their needs and will keep them 'as a shepherd keeps his flock'. When they are established once more in the land, 'they shall be radiant over the goodness of the LORD' and be satisfied with God's abundant provision.

Israel and Judah restored together

The focus in 31:15–22 is on the return of the northern kingdom of Israel, exiled in 721 BC. Jeremiah imagines Rachel, mother of Joseph and Benjamin, and therefore ancestress of the Joseph tribes Ephraim and Manasseh, weeping for her children. The Lord's command is for Rachel to stop weeping, because her children are about to 'come back to their own country' (31:15–17). Ephraim's cry, acknowledging the Lord's discipline and praying to be restored, has been heard (31:18–19). God's heart yearns for Ephraim his 'dear son' and 'darling child', and he will surely have mercy on him (31:20). Changing the imagery, another oracle summons 'virgin Israel', the 'faithless daughter' of God to return to her cities (31:21–22).

In 31:23–26 the focus turns to Judah and its cities. When the Lord restores their fortunes, there will be much material blessing, but God also promises spiritual renewal at an individual level: 'I will satisfy the weary soul, and every languishing soul I will replenish.' Both the house of Israel and the house of Judah will be sown with 'the seed of man and the seed of beast' (31:27), suggesting that the human and the animal population will be restored together. This reverses the judgment against humans and animals announced in 7:20; 21:6. Words spoken to Jeremiah at his commissioning (1:10, 12) are recalled as the Lord claims that he has 'watched over' both houses, 'to pluck up and break down, to overthrow, destroy and bring harm', and now will 'watch over them to build and to plant' (31:28; cf. 24:6–7).

A proverbial statement is quoted in 31:29–30 (cf. Ezek. 18:2), only to be rejected:

> The fathers have eaten sour grapes,
> and the children's teeth are set on edge.

Although there was a long history of disobedience to the Lord in Israel and Judah, the children were not simply being punished for the sins of their fathers. 'Inside the national covenant men were to make their individual choice of commitment to Yahweh. Each new generation had to choose afresh (Deut. 5:3).'[16] If some were saying that God was unjust to punish them for the sins of their fathers (cf. Ezek. 18:25), when they came to genuine repentance they would acknowledge their own responsibility for the judgment of God on his people (cf. Jer. 32:18–19).

---

16. Thompson, *Jeremiah*, p. 579. Williamson, *Sealed with an Oath*, p. 151, explains the apparent contradiction between 31:29–30 and 31:34 by arguing that under the New Covenant neither ancestral nor personal sins will evoke judgment. Another way of viewing this is to notice that a series of expanding promises in five prose oracles opens up the horizons of hope step by step.

The New Covenant

Jeremiah 31:31–34 develops several of the themes examined so far. Together with the affirmation of God's continuing commitment to 'the offspring of Israel' in 31:35–37, the New Covenant oracle forms a climax to the first half of the Book of Comfort. The Lord declares that he will begin again with Israel and 'restore a covenantal relationship that has been lost in the debacle of disobedience and destruction'.[17] As the creator and sustainer of the universe, he guarantees the permanence of this relationship with his people and the re-establishment of their city (31:35–40; cf. Gen. 9:16).[18]

Continuity and discontinuity

Commentators have long argued about whether the New Covenant is simply a renewal of the previous covenant or not. There is a stress on continuity with the past in 31:23–26, 35–38, but the stress in 31:27–30, 31–34 and 38–40 is on discontinuity. In these three passages, the expression 'Behold, the days are coming' introduces the note of change (vv. 27, 31, 38), expressed in promises relevant to 'the immediate post-exilic restoration as well as to the future restoration in the eschaton'.[19] The formal structure of the oracle in 31:31–34 also stresses discontinuity: 'not like the covenant' (v. 32) is followed by 'but this is the covenant' (v. 33), and 'no longer' is opposed by 'for they shall all know me' (v. 34). This suggests that

---

17. Brueggemann, *Theology*, p. 126.
18. Lundbom, *Jeremiah 21–36*, p. 488, argues that, since the Mosaic covenant was broken, what sustained Israel until the New Covenant was realized was the knowledge that the covenant made with Abraham is 'eternal and cannot be broken' (31:35–37).
19. T. Rata, *The Covenant Motif in Jeremiah's Book of Comfort: Textual and Intertextual Studies of Jeremiah 30–33*, SBL 105 (New York: Peter Lang, 2007), p. 40. Against Rata, p. 43, the expression 'after those days' (31:33) is resumptive and does not refer to 'some point later than the first time the covenant is initiated'.

the word 'new' in the expression 'new covenant' indicates 'radical discontinuity'.[20]

In favour of the renewal argument, there is to be a restoration of the fundamental relationship between God and 'the house of Israel and the house of Judah', expressed in the familiar words 'I will be their God, and they will be my people' (v. 33; cf. 7:23; 11:4; 30:22; Exod. 6:7; 19:5; Lev. 26:12; Deut. 29:13; Ezek. 36:28). Moreover, it appears that 'the shape of the new covenant relationship is according to the Torah':[21] God promises literally to put his law 'within them' and to 'write it on their hearts' (v. 33).[22] Furthermore, God finds fault with his people and not with the Mosaic covenant itself (v. 32; cf. Heb. 8:8).

Nevertheless, the accusation against the people ('my covenant that they broke') does highlight the failure of the covenant to deal adequately with the problem of human sin. Jeremiah's accusation also serves to 'illumine the acts and nature of the covenant God'.[23] The focus in verse 32 is on the love and faithfulness of the Lord, expressed historically in saving the Israelites ('I took them by the hand to bring them out of the land of Egypt'), and persisting in his

---

20. A. G. Shead, 'The New Covenant and Pauline Hermeneutics', in P. Bolt and M. Thompson (eds.), *The Gospel to the Nations: Perspectives on Paul's Mission* (Leicester: Apollos, 2000), p. 37. Shead, p. 41, notes that the Hebrew word *ḥădāšâ* could mean 'renewed' (cf. Lam. 3:23), but this is a rare case and the usual sense is radical newness (cf. Jer. 31:22). Cf. Lundbom, *Jeremiah 21–36*, p. 466; Williamson, *Sealed with an Oath*, pp. 148–149, 152–153.

21. Brueggemann, *Theology*, p. 127 (emphasis removed). However, Jeremiah's teaching about the transforming work of God in 3:15–18 suggests that Brueggemann too narrowly envisages the New Covenant shaping a people simply 'in obedience to the commands of Sinai'. The law of God will be applied in a new way in the reconstituted Israel, as 31:34 implies with its promise of a definitive forgiveness of sins.

22. The singular *libbām* (their heart) is significant: the heart of the people collectively will be changed (cf. 32:39). NIV ('I will put my law in their minds and write it on their hearts') follows the Greek version (Jer. 38:33 LXX), which parallels mind with heart.

23. Shead, 'New Covenant', pp. 37–38.

relationship with them ('I was their husband'),[24] even though they continued to rebel against him (cf. 31:2–3). The surprising implication is that the New Covenant will surpass the former covenant in demonstrating the love and faithfulness of God! 'The newness of this covenant will consist in what God does to surpass his acts of old.'[25] The next two verses explain how radically different the outcome will be.

Renewed in heart

God undertakes to write his words, not on stone tablets as before (Exod. 31:18; 34:28), but to put his law 'within them' and to write it 'on their hearts' (v. 33; cf. 24:7; 32:39).[26] In ancient Hebrew thinking, the 'will' took up residence in the 'heart', so if the law is written on the heart 'people will have to obey it'.[27] This is another way of saying that the Lord would fulfil his promise to circumcise the heart of his people, so that they might love him wholeheartedly and live (Deut. 30:6). Only such radical surgery could overcome their stubborn disobedience and rebellion against God.

Significantly, the covenant formula follows ('And I will be their God, and they shall be my people'), with the order of the parties

---

24. Commentators debate whether the expression here (bāʿaltî) and in 3:14 is an image from marriage or whether the expression should be rendered, 'I was their master'. Either way, the meaning is that God remained committed to them in the face of their unfaithfulness to him.

25. Shead, 'New Covenant', p. 38. The language of 'cutting' (kārattî) a covenant is normally used for the establishment of a new covenant (Shead, p. 41; Rata, *Covenant Motif*, pp. 46–47).

26. The idea that God freely 'gives' his law is conveyed by the verb nātattî (cf. 32:39). Internalization of the law is first expressed by bĕqirbām (in their inward parts), where the noun refers to the inner organs, including the heart and the stomach, though with a plurality of persons the expression can mean 'among them' (BDB). The internalization of the law is then expressed by God's intention to 'write it upon their heart' (wĕʿal-libbām ʾektăbennâ). But note the way the effect of this promise is expressed in 32:39–40.

27. Lundbom, *Jeremiah 21–36*, p. 469. Cf. 3:10; 29:13.

reversed to highlight the initiative of God (contrast 24:7; 30:22; 32:38). Giving his law to his people in this new way would make it possible for the relationship to be resumed and maintained. There is no conditional 'if' clause, as in Exodus 19:5, but the promise of Jeremiah 31:33 both enables and obliges the recipients 'to conform to the will of God and live indeed as those who are God's people'.[28] The sin of God's people was 'engraved on the tablet of their heart' (17:1), but the Lord would overwrite this with the revelation of his will and give them the desire to obey (32:39–40, to 'fear' God for ever). This gift would be for his people collectively, not just for isolated individuals, so that they might function effectively as the covenant community.

A new knowledge of God

The universality of this transforming work is expressed when the Lord declares, 'no longer shall each one teach his neighbour and each his brother, saying, "Know the LORD," for they shall all know me, from the least of them to the greatest' (31:34a). Previous promises that shepherds would feed the people with knowledge and understanding (3:15; 23:4) are not negated here. The meaning is that neighbours and friends across the whole spectrum of the community would share the same knowledge of God and his will and express that knowledge in godly behaviour.[29] In 8:22 – 9:9 Jeremiah denounces the deceit and oppression of neighbours who do not know the Lord (cf. 22:13–17). But in 31:34 he envisages that the New Covenant will be 'an answer to the problem of a disintegrated society'.[30] The verb 'know' in this context 'probably carries its most profound connotation, the intimate personal knowledge which arises

---

28. Williamson, *Sealed with an Oath*, 154. Williamson observes that this internalization of the law in the entire community of God's people is perhaps 'the most radical distinctive of the new covenant'.

29. Shead, 'New Covenant', p. 39, describes 31:34a as 'a rhetorical device to show the universality of this unmediated knowledge, rather than a rejection of leadership and teaching *per se*'. Cf. Lundbom, *Jeremiah 21–36*, p. 470.

30. J. G. McConville, *NIDOTTE* 4:765. Cf. 32:39–40.

between two persons who are committed wholly to one another in a relationship that touches mind, emotion, and will'.[31]

The 'all' who will know the Lord are 'the house of Israel' and 'the house of Judah' (vv. 31, 33). As noted previously, Jeremiah envisages a reunification of the elect from northern and southern kingdoms (e.g. 3:14–18; 23:6; 31:27–30; 50:4–5). However, this restored remnant would also include representatives from the nations, who gather to the Lord in Jerusalem (3:17), learn the ways of God's people (12:16), and confess the worthlessness of their idolatry (16:19–21). The nations are not mentioned specifically in the prophecy of the New Covenant, but a wider reading of Jeremiah suggests that the benefits promised to renewed Israel apply to Gentiles who are caught up in God's saving plan.

Definitive forgiveness

The Sinai covenant was established by God after his rescue of the Israelites from captivity in Egypt (Exod. 19:1–6). Jeremiah 31:34 suggests that the New Covenant will be established by another act of divine grace: God's people will know and relate to him in a new way, 'because' (*kî*) he 'will forgive their iniquity' (*'eslaḥ la'ăwōnām*) and 'will remember their sin no more' (*lĕḥaṭṭā'tām lō' 'ezkār-'ôd*).[32] Of course, God's forgiveness was known and experienced by his people prior to this (e.g. Exod. 34:6–7; Lev. 4:20, 26, 31, 35; Pss 51:1–9; 130:3–4).[33] But Israel and Judah had come under the curse of the covenant, which involved exile and the destruction of everything

---

31. Thompson, *Jeremiah*, p. 581. T. E. Fretheim, *NIDOTTE* 2:413, observes that 'to know God is to be in a right relationship with him, with characteristics of love, trust, respect, and open communication'.

32. There is a poetic couplet at the end of v. 34, with the second clause ('I will remember their sin no more') explaining more fully the significance of the first clause ('I will forgive their iniquity'). The promise not to remember their sin makes the definitive character of this forgiveness clearer.

33. The verb *slḥ* (forgive) is used primarily in cultic contexts in the OT. It occurs eight times in the prophetic literature, mostly in Jeremiah. The theme of unconditional forgiveness appears to be articulated in Jer. 31:34 for the first time in Scripture. Cf. J. P. J. Olivier, *NIDOTTE* 3:259–264.

they held dear (11:9–13; 13:15–27; cf. Deut. 28:25–68). Many must have wondered whether forgiveness would ever be possible again.

Jeremiah insisted that judgment would come, but God would not make a full end of his people. He would show mercy in restoring, forgiving and cleansing a remnant 'from all the guilt of their sin . . . and rebellion' (33:8). So decisively would he deal with the problem that their sin would not be remembered by him or be held against them any longer.[34] When God 'remembers' sin he punishes it (14:10); so when he promises *not* to remember sin (31:34), he indicates that he will no longer act in judgment against it. Jeremiah had declared that 'everyone shall die for his own sin' (31:30), but now he proclaims a release from that penalty.

No indication is given about the means by which God's justice would be satisfied or human guilt atoned for. An unprecedented act of divine grace is signalled in 31:34. Return from exile and the re-establishment of the people in the Promised Land could be regarded as a first expression of this, but Jeremiah's vision for the restoration indicates much more. Pardon for sins past, present and future would seem to be necessary to keep God's people in the promised relationship and maintain the covenant. The law of Moses made various provisions for atonement, but Jeremiah does not suggest that the revival of such ritual in the Jerusalem temple would be the means by which the heart of the people might be changed.[35]

Contemplating the rebellion of God's people and the judgment of the exile, Isaiah 52:13 – 53:12 proclaims the need for the substitutionary death of the Servant of the Lord to bring reconciliation

---

34. Shead, 'New Covenant', pp. 40–41, argues persuasively against the view that 31:34 is predicting sinlessness in the renewed people of God. In 50:20 sin is not 'found' in the remnant because God will 'pardon' them.

35. Although Jer. 33:18 predicts the restoration of the Levitical priesthood and their sacrificial ministry, this is linked to the restoration of Davidic kingship in some new mode of operation. As indicated in 3:15–17, a transformation of worship will take place, involving the fulfilment of realities to which the ancient rituals pointed. Jeremiah speaks about a discontinuous future, using categories familiar from the past.

between God and his people. In various ways, as we shall see, New Testament writers point to the fulfilment of such expectations in the death of Jesus and link this to the promise of Jeremiah 31:34.

So the unbreakable character of the New Covenant rests on several interconnected promises. God will provide a definitive forgiveness of sins, requiring no further judgment and bringing a new knowledge of God as gracious and faithful. This knowledge will bring about a profound change of heart in his people. Foundationally, 'the ability of sin to disrupt the relationship is made obsolete by the outstanding announcement that God will not remember sins and their effects on the relationship'.[36] Radical forgiveness is the basis for the promised spiritual and moral transformation of the people.

Further messages of hope

Chapters 32–33 form the second half of the Book of Comfort. Although entirely in prose, these chapters link with themes in the diverse oracles of chapters 30–31. In the opening narrative, God commands Jeremiah to buy a field at Anathoth, even though this seems to contradict his message about the imminent captivity of the land by the Chaldeans (32:1–8). The Lord declares that this purchase and the preservation of the deeds are a sign that 'houses and fields and vineyards shall again be bought in this land' (32:9–15; cf. 32:43–44). But Jeremiah queries the command (32:25) and the rest of the chapter contains the Lord's response to Jeremiah's prayer.[37]

---

36. J. A. Dearman, *Jeremiah and Lamentations*, NIVAC (Grand Rapids: Zondervan, 2002), p. 287.

37. Lundbom, *Jeremiah 21–36*, p. 499, notes the parallel between 31:31–34 (Oracle on the New Covenant) and 32:36–41 (Oracle on the Eternal Covenant), followed by 31:38–40 (Oracle on the Rebuilding of Jerusalem) and 32:42–44 (Oracle on Renewed Field Purchases in Benjamin and Judah).

A people united in the fear of the Lord

God confirms that he is giving the city of Jerusalem over to judgment by the Chaldeans and recalls the sins of Judah that have provoked him to anger (32:26–35). At the same time, he confirms his intention to gather together his people from various countries and bring them back to Jerusalem to dwell in safety (32:36–37). The covenantal implications of this restoration are then re-expressed.

First, there is a repetition of the foundational promise 'they shall be my people, and I will be their God' (32:38). Secondly, there is the promise to 'give them one heart and one way, that they may fear me for ever, for their own good and the good of their children after them' (32:39). Thirdly, there is the promise that God will make with them 'an everlasting covenant', that he will 'not turn away from doing good to them' (32:40). This is linked to the preceding promise with the words 'I will put the fear of me in their hearts, that they may not turn from me.' Finally, there is the assurance that God will 'rejoice in doing them good, and I will plant them in this land in faithfulness, with all my heart and all my soul' (32:41).

Parallel with the prophecy of the New Covenant, this passage speaks about the gift of 'one heart and one way', instead of promising that God will put his law within them and write it on their heart.[38] A change of heart is indicated by the words 'that they may fear me for ever', and the unity of the people in their devotion to God is expressed by repetition of the word 'one'.[39] In effect, 32:39 expresses the consequence of the law being written on the heart.[40] This trans-formation of the people, coupled with God's promise not to turn

38. Williamson, *Sealed with an Oath*, p. 165, provides a helpful table, comparing 31:31–34 and 32:37–41. Lundbom, *Jeremiah 21–36*, p. 519, notes that the promise to give 'singleness of mind and of purpose' is significant in view of the fact that 'it was duplicity in worship that led to a breakdown of the Sinai covenant and the crisis that the people are now in'.

39. Appropriate fear or respect for God was meant to keep Israel from sinning (Exod. 20:20). Here it would unite them in service to the Lord and keep them from turning away from him.

40. Thompson, *Jeremiah*, p. 596, views the references to the fear of the Lord in 32:39–40 as a substitute for the knowledge of the Lord in 31:34.

away from doing good to them, explains how the New Covenant can be everlasting (cf. 50:5; Isa. 55:3; Ezek. 16:60; 37:26), an idea that is only implicit in 31:31–40. Although there is no promise of forgiveness here (cf. 33:8; 50:20), the restoration of the people in material and spiritual terms implies this (32:42–44).[41]

Health and healing for God's people

Further words to Jeremiah about the future are linked with the preceding messages (33:1). Despite the judgment that is coming upon the city (33:2–5), God promises to bring it 'health and healing', saying, 'I will heal them and reveal to them abundance of prosperity and security' (33:6; cf. 30:17). Healing is first expressed in terms of restoring the fortunes of Judah and Israel and rebuilding them 'as they were at first' (33:7). But the relational aspect of this healing is stressed with a promise of cleansing and forgiveness: 'I will cleanse them from all the guilt of their sin against me, and I will forgive all the guilt of their sin and rebellion against me' (33:8; cf. 31:34; Ezek. 36:25–26).

Transformed behaviour on the part of the nations is then signalled by the promise that

> this city shall be to me a name of joy, a praise and a glory before all the nations of the earth who shall hear of all the good that I do for them. They shall fear and tremble because of all the good and all the prosperity I provide for it. (33:9)

This fear of the Lord is perhaps a preliminary to the gathering of representatives from the nations to Jerusalem, as predicted in 3:17; 12:16; 16:19–20.[42]

The transformation of land and people is proclaimed once more in 33:10–13. Happy voices will be heard in the cities of Judah and

---

41. Economic prosperity in 32:42–44 is a development of the material aspect of the comprehensive restoration portrayed in 30:17–21; 31:4–14, 23–28.

42. Lundbom, *Jeremiah 21–36*, p. 533, suggests that 'the nations will tremble – so much so that they may come themselves to worship Yahweh'.

the streets of Jerusalem again, as people marry and rejoice in God's goodness to his people (contrast 7:34; 16:9; 25:10). A renewal of worship at the temple is indicated by the promise that they will bring thank offerings to the house of the Lord, singing his praise (cf. 17:26).

Kingship and priesthood renewed

God's promise to raise up 'a righteous Branch' from the line of David, to 'execute justice and righteousness in the land', is reiterated in 33:14–16 (cf. 23:5–6; Isa. 4:2; Zech. 3:8; 6:12) with a specific application to the restoration of Judah and Jerusalem.[43] A Davidic king will rule as God's agent, saving his people and enabling them to dwell securely in the city whose name will proclaim that 'The LORD is our righteousness.' This is guaranteed by the Lord's covenant with the house of David, which is alluded to with the claim that 'David shall never lack a man to sit on the throne of the house of Israel' (33:17; cf. 2 Sam. 7:12–16; 1 Kgs 2:4; 8:25; Ps. 89:35–37). The Levitical priesthood receives a parallel assurance: 'the Levitical priests shall never lack a man in my presence to offer burnt offerings, to burn grain offerings, and to make sacrifices for ever' (33:18; cf. Num. 25:11–13). So even if kings and priests perish in the exile and city and temple are destroyed, God will renew these institutions in some way for the benefit of his people.[44]

It appears from 3:16–18 that the renewal of worship in Jerusalem will not involve a literal re-establishment of temple, priesthood and sacrifice. If the ark of the covenant is not remade and believers from the nations can gather in Jerusalem 'to the presence of the LORD' without that important symbol being present, it is likely that

---

43. Although 33:14–26 is missing from the Greek version of Jeremiah, the Hebrew text is broadly consistent with previous oracles of hope.

44. The Levitical priesthood will be renewed when the Davidic kingship is renewed, and the eternal operation of the former (*kol-ḥayyāmîm*, 'for ever') is guaranteed by the promise of perpetual rule to the house of David. Both institutions become linked to the New Covenant by this emphasis on eternal or perpetual operation (cf. 32:39, *kol-ḥayyāmîm*). Cf. Sirach 45.23–26.

priesthood and sacrifice will operate in an entirely new way. Hebrews 5 – 10 shows how the Levitical priesthood and its functions are fulfilled by Jesus, who as the promised Davidic king becomes 'a priest for ever after the order of Melchizedek' (Ps. 110:4).[45]

God's commitment to maintain his covenant with David and his covenant with the Levitical priests is linked to his 'covenant' with the day and night (33:19–22; cf. Ps. 89:19–37). This is similar to the promise in 31:35–37 that the Lord's commitment to Israel is as certain as his maintenance of the fixed order of creation. God's guarantee is extended to include 'the two clans that he chose', collectively described as 'the offspring of Jacob' and 'the offspring of Abraham, Isaac, and Jacob' (33:23–26). So within the space of a few verses there is an allusion to the covenants with the patriarchs, with the Levitical priests, and with David, to assure Jeremiah's contemporaries of God's continuing commitment to his promises, even through the judgment of exile and the radical changes to come. By implication, each of these covenants is reaffirmed and fulfilled in the establishment of the New Covenant, though the outcome will be different from the original form of these institutions.[46]

Parallels in other prophetic books

Hosea uses somewhat similar language in his own historical, literary and theological context, when he speaks of the Lord's mercy in restoring the covenant relationship with his people and betrothing

---

45. In D. G. Peterson, *Hebrews and Perfection: An Examination of the Concept of Perfection in the 'Epistle to the Hebrews'*, SNTSMS 47 (Cambridge: Cambridge University Press, 1982), pp. 191–195, I argue that in Hebrews Jesus fulfils the type of Aaron's high priesthood as priest 'after the order of Melchizedek'.

46. Cf. Rata, *Covenant Motif*, pp. 85, 88. Lundbom, *Jeremiah 21–36*, p. 545, observes that 'with the Sinai covenant broken, it is the Abrahamic covenant – and also by implication the Davidic covenant – that will preserve Israel until the new and eternal covenant takes effect'.

Israel to him for ever 'in righteousness and in justice, in steadfast love and in mercy' (2:14–23).[47]

Isaiah identifies the Servant of the Lord as 'a covenant for the people' (42:6; 49:8), whose role is to be 'the agent and guarantor of God's covenant' for Israel and the nations.[48] Isaiah goes on to proclaim that God will gather his people together again 'with ever-lasting love': his steadfast love will not depart from them and his 'covenant of peace' shall not be removed (54:4–10). Their children shall all be 'taught by the LORD' and enjoy peace, because they are established in righteousness and far from oppression (54:13–14). God will make with his people 'an everlasting covenant' (55:3; 61:8),[49] and the beneficiaries will include 'foreigners who join themselves to the LORD' (56:3–8). This covenant will be everlasting because

> 'My Spirit that is upon you, and my words that I have put in your mouth, shall not depart out of your mouth, or out of the mouth of your offspring, or out of the mouth of your children's offspring,' says the LORD, from this time forth and for evermore. (59:21; cf. 44:3)

A certain parallel with the prophecy of Joel 2:28–29 can be seen in this promise.

Ezekiel's first prophecy of restoration includes God's promise to return the exiles to their land, to remove everything that is abhorrent to him (11:17–18), and to renew the people spiritually:

> I will give them one heart, and a new spirit I will put within them. I will remove the heart of stone from their flesh and give them a heart of

---

47. Lundbom, *Jeremiah 21–36*, pp. 371–374, lists verbal parallels between Jer. 30 – 31 and the prophecies of Hosea and Isaiah. Williamson, *Sealed with an Oath*, pp. 174–179, comments on Dan. 9:24–27; Hos. 2:14–23; Mal. 3:1.
48. Williamson, *Sealed with an Oath*, p. 160. Cf. Lundbom, *Jeremiah 21–36*, p. 520.
49. Noting allusions to the covenants with Noah, Abraham, Israel and David in Isa. 54 – 55, Williamson, *Sealed with an Oath*, p. 161, suggests that this covenant 'constitutes the climactic covenant in which all the major divine–human covenants find their ultimate fulfilment'.

flesh, that they may walk in my statutes and keep my rules and obey them. And they shall be my people, and I will be their God. (11:19–20; cf. 36:26–28)

Israel's breaking of the Sinai covenant is explicitly mentioned in Ezekiel 16:59–63, before the Lord promises to establish for his people 'an everlasting covenant' (16:60; 37:26). The parallels with Jeremiah 31:31–34 can be seen as God promises 'a quickening of the memory . . . an intense sense of shame . . . a profound recognition of Yahweh . . . a full atonement for sin'.[50]

Like Isaiah, Ezekiel speaks of this everlasting covenant as 'a covenant of peace', involving an end to God's judgment and the gift of security, harmony, and fulfilment in a renewed creation (34:25–31). As with Jeremiah, this restoration is associated with the blessing of a truly Davidic king, 'who would prove to be the shepherd Yahweh intended'.[51] The divine action of gathering the exiles, cleansing the land and renewing the people is stressed again in 36:22–38 (cf. 11:16–20). Ezekiel parallels Jeremiah's promise of forgiveness with the assurance of divine cleansing. He goes on to promise the gift of a new heart and a new spirit, when God replaces their 'heart of stone' with 'a heart of flesh' and puts *his* Spirit within them (cf. Joel 2:28–29). So spiritual heart surgery, together with an infusion of God's Spirit, will make it possible for God's people to walk in his statutes and be careful to obey his rules.

Ezekiel 37 brings all these hopes together, predicting the 'resurrection' and renewal of Israel by God's Spirit (vv. 1–14), the reunification of the tribes under a Davidic king (vv. 15–22, 24–25), cleansing from idolatry and every transgression (v. 23), obedience

---

50. Williamson, *Sealed with an Oath*, p. 169. Williamson argues that this unbreakable covenant is a replacement for the Sinai covenant that Israel broke.

51. Ibid., p. 170. Cf. D. I. Block, 'Bringing back David: Ezekiel's Messianic Hope', in P. E. Satterthwaite, R. S. Hess and G. J. Wenham (eds.), *The Lord's Anointed: Interpretation of Old Testament Messianic Texts* (Grand Rapids: Baker; Carlisle: Paternoster, 1995), pp. 167–188.

to God and security in the land, because God will set his sanctuary in their midst for evermore (vv. 24–28). The note of permanence is struck several times in this passage, and indications are given that the transformation of Israel will be 'the realization of the hopes held out in previous covenants'.[52]

Conclusion

Jeremiah's prophecy of a new covenant 'serves to explain how God will maintain his relationship with his people in the future and ensure that history does not simply end up repeating itself'.[53] The setting in chapters 30–31 clearly gives the oracle a climactic significance, while its main themes are developed and linked to other aspects of the promised restoration in chapters 32–33 and elsewhere. The New Covenant 'forms a centrepiece of a larger hope that includes a new act of salvation, a new Zion, and a new Davidic king'.[54] Although this New Covenant will have continuity with the Mosaic or Sinai Covenant,

> it will still be a genuinely new covenant, one that marks a new beginning in the divine–human relationship because 1) it is given without conditions, 2) it will be written in the hearts of people in a way the Sinai covenant was not (v. 33), and 3) it will be grounded in a wholly new act of divine grace, i.e., the forgiveness of sins (v. 34).[55]

When parallels in other prophetic writings are examined, it can be seen that the promise of a new covenant is variously expressed, but that there are common threads. The New Covenant will be both national and international in its effect, it will involve both continuity and discontinuity with previous divine covenants, and it will be both

---

52. Williamson, *Sealed with an Oath*, p. 173.

53. Ibid., p. 152.

54. Lundbom, *Jeremiah 21–36*, p. 466.

55. Ibid.

the climactic fulfilment of those covenants and an everlasting covenant of peace.[56]

New Testament writers draw on many of these threads, sometimes weaving together a complex of ideas to proclaim the fulfilment of New Covenant expectations. But Jeremiah 31:31–34 appears to have had a particular influence on their thinking. In part, this was because of the comprehensive nature of Jeremiah's oracle and the way in which its promises relate together and express the hopes outlined in other contexts. But Jeremiah's unique use of the expression 'a new covenant', together with the covenant structure of the oracle itself, raised important questions about the relationship of this divine provision to previous covenants. Was it merely a renewal of the Sinai Covenant or something more novel? If it was the fulfilment of the covenant made by God with Abraham and the patriarchs, what were the implications for the nations, for the law of Moses and for the life and future of national Israel?

---

56. Cf. Williamson, *Sealed with an Oath*, pp. 179–181. Susanne Lehne, *The New Covenant in Hebrews*, JSNTSS 44 (Sheffield: JSOT Press, 1990), pp. 35–61, examines passages from later Jewish writings, which at first glance appear to reflect Jeremiah's prophecy of a new covenant. However, apart from the Dead Sea Scrolls, these all reflect a return to the old covenantal relationship with God.

2. ISRAEL AND THE NATIONS RENEWED

At first glance, Luke's Gospel and the Acts of the Apostles seem to say little about the promised New Covenant. Luke's teaching about salvation is very much influenced by Isaiah's predictions, though the focus on repentance and the forgiveness of sins certainly echoes Jeremiah's concerns.[1] Indeed, it is clear from the Last Supper saying in Luke 22:20 that Jeremiah's oracle provides an interpretative key to the ministry of Jesus. Only in Luke's account does Jesus say 'this cup that is poured out for you is the new covenant in my blood'. Although this claim is not immediately linked to forgiveness (cf. Matt. 26:28), at the climax of Luke's Gospel Jesus commissions his disciples to proclaim repentance and forgiveness of sins to all nations in his name, beginning from Jerusalem (24:47). This proclamation is clearly related to his death and resurrection in fulfilment of Scripture (24:45–46).

---

1. Cf. D. W. Pao, *Acts and the Isaianic New Exodus* (Grand Rapids: Baker Academic, 2000), pp. 70–110.

In Acts, the offer of repentance and forgiveness in the name of Jesus is made to Jews, proselytes and Gentiles everywhere. The covenantal basis of this offer is made clear in various ways (e.g. 2:38–39; 3:19–26; 13:38–39; 20:28, 32), climaxing in Paul's final defence speech, which recalls the charge by the risen Lord to offer to Jews and Gentiles, 'forgiveness of sins and a place among those who are sanctified by faith in me' (26:18). So in his second volume Luke shows how obedience to the commission of Jesus brings into existence a new people of God, formed by the gospel that effects transformation.

Fundamentally, Luke-Acts is concerned to portray the fulfilment of God's plan of redemption for Israel and the nations. The benefits of Christ's saving work are shown to be a definitive release from the penalty and power of sin and a new pattern of devotion and service to God, determined not by the law of Moses but by the Holy Spirit. These blessings are presented in narratives and speeches, with constant reference to the way in which they fulfil a range of prophetic predictions.

A remnant in waiting

Luke's opening chapters introduce a number of godly Israelites who are 'waiting for the consolation of Israel' (2:25) or 'waiting for the redemption of Jerusalem' (2:38; cf. 23:50–51; 24:21). Their expectations are critical for understanding the significance of what happens in subsequent narratives.

Redemption at hand
Zechariah is told about the birth of a son who will be the Elijah figure predicted by the prophets, sent 'to turn the hearts of the fathers to the children, and the disobedient to the wisdom of the just, to make ready for the Lord a people prepared' (1:16–17; cf. Isa. 40:3–5; Mal. 3:1–4; 4:5–6). This task is later described as preparing a way for the Lord (1:76; 3:4; 7:27): 'John prepares the Lord's way by preparing a repentant people, whose hearts have turned and who are ready to

receive their Lord.'[2] The giving of 'one heart and one way', enabling God's people to fear him for ever (Jer. 32:39), begins with the ministry of the Baptist. As we shall see, there is a profound interest in Luke-Acts in the way people respond to God in their hearts.

When John is born, Zechariah is filled with the Holy Spirit and prophesies about the significance of this moment in Israel's history. Speaking with absolute confidence about what is to happen, he declares that God has 'visited and redeemed his people' and has raised up the Davidic ruler promised by the prophets (1:68–69; cf. Jer. 23:5–6).[3] The Messiah will deliver God's people from their enemies and fulfil the covenant promises initially made to Abraham, enabling his people to 'serve him without fear, in holiness and righteousness before him all our days' (1:70–75; cf. Acts 7:5–7). This transformation into a righteous, worshipping community recalls promises such as Jeremiah 3:16–18; 33:14–22.

As the prophet who will 'go before the Lord to prepare his ways', John gives 'knowledge' or experience of salvation to his people 'in the forgiveness of their sins' (1:76–77). Salvation will be accomplished by God's merciful visitation,

> to give light to those who sit in darkness and in the shadow of death,
> to guide our feet into the way of peace.
>
> (1:78–79; cf. Isa. 9:2–7)[4]

Zechariah's prophecy echoes the expectation of Isaiah, Jeremiah and others about the re-establishment of Davidic rule, the spiritual

---

2. R. C. Tannehill, *The Narrative Unity of Luke-Acts: A Literary Interpretation*. Vol. 1: *The Gospel According to Luke* (Philadelphia: Fortress, 1986), p. 24.

3. God has literally 'made redemption' (1:68, *epoiēsen lytrōsin*) for his people, thus fulfilling the hope of godly Israelites who believed the words of the prophets (2:38; 24:21; cf. 21:28 [*apolytrōsis*]). The parallel terminology of salvation is used more extensively throughout Luke-Acts.

4. J. Nolland, *Luke 1–9:20*, WBC 35A (Dallas: Word, 1989), p. 92, observes that 'John in a preliminary and Jesus in an ultimate way will be the instruments of the end-time outpouring of the tender mercies of God (v. 78).'

renewal of God's people and the fulfilment of God's covenant promises. But Zechariah does not anticipate the way Israel will reject her king and suffer the judgment of God on Jerusalem and its people (cf. Luke 13:34–35; 19:41–44; 21:20–24; 23:27–31).

The redeemer revealed

Gabriel's revelation to Mary about the birth of Jesus indicates that he will be more than a prophet like John. As 'the Son of the Most High', the Lord God will 'give to him the throne of his father David, and he will reign over the house of Jacob for ever, and of his kingdom there will be no end' (1:32–33; cf. 2 Sam. 7:12–16; Isa. 9:6–7; Jer. 23:5–6; 33:14–26). Jesus is God's Son in the sense that he is the promised Davidic Messiah, who is miraculously conceived (1:34–35; cf. Isa. 7:14). The hope that he will succeed to David's throne and achieve the redemption of God's people is repeated in the angelic announcement at the birth of Jesus (2:10–11).

Meanwhile, the significance of God's visitation is proclaimed in Mary's Song. The gift of a son is a sign of God's mercy towards those who fear him (1:46–51). The Lord scatters the proud 'in the thoughts of their hearts' and brings down the mighty from their thrones, but he exalts his humble servants and fills the hungry with good things (cf. 6:20–26; 10:21; 13:25–30).[5] His merciful intervention in the life of Mary is a sign of his intention to help his servant Israel, in faithfulness to his covenant promises (1:51–55).

Simeon's first utterance echoes the joy and hope of Zechariah's prophecy, but adds the prediction that the salvation God has prepared will be

a light for revelation to the Gentiles,
and for glory to your people Israel.
(2:29–32; cf. Isa. 40:5; 42:6; 46:13; 49:6; 52:9–10)

---

5. Tannehill, *Luke*, pp. 29–31, shows how the pattern of reversal in Mary's song introduces a motif that is highlighted in the teaching of Jesus and influences the way the gospel is presented in Acts.

This universalism is tempered in Simeon's second utterance, which declares that 'this child is appointed for the fall and rising of many in Israel, and for a sign that is opposed' (2:34). Jesus will bring division among the people and Mary will ultimately stand with her son as one opposed ('a sword will pass through your own soul also', my tr.).[6] Opposition to Jesus will reveal the true state of affairs in the hearts of many (2:35). This is illustrated in a number of ways as Luke's narrative progresses (e.g. 5:21–22; 6:8; 9:46–47; 20:14; 22:1–6).

Redemption proclaimed

John the Baptist
The word of God comes to John as it did to Jeremiah, leading him to preach a baptism of repentance 'for the forgiveness of sins' (3:3), and to call for transformed behaviour across the spectrum of Judean society (3:7–14; cf. Jer. 3:12–18; 4:1–4). But the difference for John is the imminent coming of God and the redemption he has promised. By responding appropriately to John's message, his contemporaries show themselves to be part of the faithful remnant, ready to meet their Lord and experience the benefits of eschatological salvation.

A substantial quotation from Isaiah 40:3–5 in Luke 3:4–6 interprets John's mission and 'reveals the purpose of God which underlies the whole narrative of Luke-Acts'.[7] Images of road building in Isaiah's prophecy are fulfilled in John's call for repentance. The Baptist addresses all Israel with his message and the expectation is that the messianic salvation will ultimately be 'seen' or experienced by 'all flesh', meaning all peoples. But, as John's ministry confirms, not everyone will repent and receive the promised salvation. John questions the motives of those who come for baptism and calls for

---

6. Nolland, *Luke 1–9:20*, p. 122, rightly suggests that 'a sword will pass through your own soul also' refers to the fact that Mary will suffer the loss of her son in death, when the opposition to him has reached its climax.

7. Tannehill, *Luke*, p. 47.

them to produce 'fruits in keeping with repentance' (3:8).[8] Those who fail to repent are warned of God's approaching wrath (3:7, 9, 17). A process of divine election begins with the preaching of John and extends through the ministry of Jesus and his disciples to the nations (cf. Acts 13:48; 16:14; 18:10; 28:23–28).

As John preaches to the crowds, the definitive forgiveness of sins that Jesus makes possible lies in the future. But its benefits can be secured by a baptism expressing repentance 'for the forgiveness of sins' (3:3, *eis aphesin hamartiōn*).[9] Even the prospect of such forgiveness can be the basis for release from sin's control. Yet John acknowledges that he is not able to deliver what the Christ will bring. Only the one who comes after John, who is mightier than he is, will be able to baptize 'with the Holy Spirit and with fire' (3:16). As one mightily endowed with the Holy Spirit, he will cleanse the penitent and bring judgment on the godless.[10]

Jesus empowered by the Spirit

Jesus is empowered by the Spirit as God's messianic Son and as the Servant of the Lord, to accomplish the promised cleansing and renewal of his people (3:21–22; cf. Ps. 2:7; Isa. 42:1–2). 'Full of the Holy Spirit', he is led by the Spirit into the wilderness, to be tested by the devil (4:1–13).

---

8. These 'fruits' include radical generosity and scrupulous honesty (3:10–14). It is interesting to note that Jesus calls for similar expressions of true repentance (6:27–36, 43–45; 12:33–34; 14:12–14; 16:9; 18:22). When Zacchaeus repents, he demonstrates by such behaviour that he has truly received the salvation Jesus offers (19:8–9).

9. So the baptism of John is both a means of expressing repentance and of seeking forgiveness from God. Nolland, *Luke 1–9:20*, p. 141, argues that 'in line with OT prophetic symbolism (e.g. Ezek 4–5), John uses the waters of the Jordan to effect the eschatologically promised washing away of sin'. Cf. Isa. 4:4; Jer. 33:8; Ezek. 36:25–26, 33; 37:23.

10. Cf. J. D. G. Dunn, *Baptism in the Holy Spirit* (London: SCM, 1970), pp. 8–14, as modified by M. M. B. Turner, *Power from on High: The Spirit in Israel's Restoration and Witness in Luke-Acts* (Sheffield: Sheffield Academic, 1996), pp. 177–180, 183–186.

Essentially this is a story about the beginnings of Israel's restoration, a 'New Exodus' begun in her messianic representative through an ordeal/ contest with Satan (in which Jesus emerges as the victorious Isaianic servant warrior).[11]

Following this encounter, Jesus returns to Galilee 'in the power of the Spirit', to begin his public ministry (4:14–15). In a sermon preached in Nazareth, he outlines the significance of his baptismal reception of the Spirit and reveals the divine agenda for his mission (4:16–30). Jesus reads most of Isaiah 61:1–2, with words from Isaiah 58:6 added as a midrashic or interpretative gloss ('to set at liberty those who are oppressed').[12] He then declares to the hushed synagogue, 'Today this Scripture has been fulfilled in your hearing.' Jesus claims to have been anointed by the Spirit for the prophetic task of announcing the promised restoration of Israel and bringing it into effect.

God is powerfully present, in his Spirit-anointed servant, to free his people from their wretched state of 'slave-poverty', 'captive-exile', 'blindness' and 'oppression', and to shepherd them along 'the way' towards Zion's restoration.[13]

'Release' (*aphesis*) is to be enacted through *proclamation*: evangelizing 'the poor' is the primary description of Jesus' task (cf. 4:43; 7:22; 8:1). This is expounded in the clauses that follow:

---

11. Turner, *Power*, p. 204. Jesus was tested much as Israel was in the wilderness, but where Israel failed, Jesus proved faithful to God and to his revealed will.

12. Turner, *Power*, pp. 215–226, argues persuasively that the citation as we have it belongs fundamentally to Luke's source, not to his own editorial activity. Cf. D. P. Seccombe, *Possessions and the Poor in Luke-Acts* (Linz: SNTU, 1982), pp. 44–54.

13. Turner, *Power*, p. 249. Turner, pp. 233–250, argues that Luke 4:16–30 portrays Jesus as the messianic prophet like Moses, who inaugurates the New Exodus. Cf. Luke 7:16; 24:19; Acts 3:22–23; 7:22, 37. The Davidic Christology in Luke's earlier chapters is a complementary way of describing Jesus.

to proclaim liberty to the captives
and recovering of sight to the blind,
to set at liberty those who are oppressed,
to proclaim the year of the Lord's favour.
(4:18–19)

The poor appear to be the people of Israel, 'understood in terms of their great need of healing, understanding, forgiveness, freedom and peace; in short, their need of salvation'.[14] Both a literal and a spiritualized application of the terms in Isaiah's prophecy emerge in Luke's account of Jesus' ministry: 'spiritual restoration, moral transformation, rescue from demonic oppression, and release from illness and disability'.[15]

Elsewhere in Luke-Acts, the Greek word *aphesis* is combined with *hamartiōn*, to indicate 'release from sins' or 'forgiveness of sins', but here the unmarked or simple meaning of the noun is 'release' or 'freedom'. Luke uses a term widely employed in connection with the Jubilee regulations in Leviticus 25 (LXX) and related texts, but applies it to a new liberation or redemption of God's people from captivity (cf. 1:68; 2:38; 21:28; 24:21).[16] Luke's understanding of the way 'release' was effected by the ministry of Jesus is indicated in what follows.

14. Seccombe, *Possessions*, p. 66. Cf. Nolland, *Luke 1–9:20*, p. 197; Turner, *Power*, p. 250.

15. Nolland, *Luke 1–9:20*, p. 202. Nolland rightly argues that the Jubilee release in the Isaiah texts is not simply spiritualized into the forgiveness of sins, 'but neither can it be resolved into a program of social reform'.

16. The verb *aphienai* means 'to send off, release, let go' and in the LXX it is sometimes used for the remission of sin or guilt (e.g. Isa. 33:24; 55:7). The substantive *aphesis* is used only in the LXX in the sense of 'release', mostly with reference to the Jubilee regulations in Exod. 23:11; Lev. 25, 27; Deut. 15:1–9; Ezek. 46:17. Turner, *Power*, pp. 226–232, discusses other uses of such terminology in Jewish literature to image salvation, especially in 11QMelch.

Jesus as the agent of God's deliverance

At first, there is amazement at 'the gracious words that were coming from his mouth', but then a growing scepticism about his authority to do what he has proposed (4:22–24). When Jesus implies that, like Elijah and Elisha, he will find a better response from Gentiles, the people in the synagogue drive him out of their town and seek to destroy him (4:25–30). This initiates a pattern of rejection that culminates in his crucifixion. Unhindered for the moment, Jesus moves on to Capernaum, where he teaches with remarkable authority in the synagogue and delivers a man who is demonically possessed (4:31–37). This dramatically illustrates God's commitment to deliver Israel from sin and uncleanness (cf. Zech. 13:1–2; Luke 11:14–23; 13:10–17). Then he heals those who come to him in faith and moves on to 'preach the good news of the kingdom of God' throughout Judea (4:38–44).

Two incidents immediately highlight the centrality of forgiveness to the ministry of Jesus. When he says to a paralysed man 'your sins are forgiven', he is charged by the scribes and the Pharisees with blasphemy, since no one can forgive sins but God alone (5:17–26). But Jesus backs up his claim by healing the man and asserting that 'the Son of Man has authority on earth to forgive sins'. Implying that he is the figure in Daniel 7:13–14, who is brought before the judgment seat of God and given dominion over the nations, Jesus offers the possibility of acquittal in advance of that final assize. God has given him authority in the present both to heal and to forgive.[17]

Forgiveness is also suggested in the next incident, when Jesus calls Levi to follow him and asserts that his eating and drinking with 'tax collectors and sinners' is another aspect of his healing ministry. 'Those who are well have no need of a physician', he says, 'but those

---

17. Against alternative interpretations, I. H. Marshall, *The Gospel of Luke: A Commentary on the Greek Text*, NIGTC (Exeter: Paternoster, 1978), pp. 215–216, argues that Jesus used the expression 'the Son of Man' to speak about himself, 'to designate his authority both on earth and at the parousia'.

who are sick. I have not come to call the righteous but sinners to repentance' (5:27–32).

When John the Baptist sends his disciples to ask 'Are you the one who is to come, or shall we look for another?' Luke notes that 'in that hour he [Jesus] healed many people of diseases and plagues and evil spirits, and on many who were blind he bestowed sight' (7:18–21).[18] This prepares for Jesus' pointed response:

> Go and tell John what you have seen and heard: the blind receive their sight, the lame walk, lepers are cleansed, and the deaf hear, the dead are raised up, the poor have good news preached to them. And blessed is the one who is not offended by me. (7:22–23)

Understood in the light of various Isaianic texts (Isa. 26:19; 29:18–19; 35:5–6; 61:1), Jesus' deeds are signs that the promised era of salvation has dawned. They point to him as the agent of God's gracious deliverance, and call for continuing trust in him, even in the face of ambiguities and opposition. Although forgiveness is central to his proclamation, his mighty works point to a complete release from the consequences of sin that will be experienced in a new creation.

The motif of eschatological judgment is not absent from the teaching of Jesus (e.g. 6:24–26; 10:13–15), but the immediate focus of his ministry is on God's grace and the opportunity to receive the blessings of salvation. Since the Baptist associated the coming of the Messiah with the ultimate judgment of God (3:15–17), his question could have arisen because Jesus had failed to bring the final cataclysmic events described by the prophets. However, as Jesus draws near to Jerusalem, he makes it clear that judgment is certainly at hand (19:41–44; 20:16–18; 21:5–36).

The final incident in Luke 7 involves Jesus' encounter with a woman who appears to have been a prostitute, but who has been

---

18. The healing of a blind person is not recorded until he is on his final journey to Jerusalem (18:35–43).

transformed by experiencing his forgiveness (7:36–50). When the woman expresses her devotion to Jesus, the narrative implies that those who have been forgiven much will love much. Previous narratives have also suggested that forgiveness makes repentance possible, and repentance leads to moral transformation (3:3–14; 5:17–26, 27–32; cf. 19:1–10).[19] 'Release from sins' (*aphesis hamartiōn*) effects a deliverance from sin's penalty, and makes possible a life of love and obedience to God's will.

Transformation and the renewal of hearts

In the midst of these narratives of transformation, Jesus' teaching about radical change emerges in encounters with different groups of people. Challenging the restrictive views of the Pharisees on fasting (5:33–38) and the sabbath (6:1–11), he implies that a new era in God's relationship with Israel has begun. Crowds gather from everywhere to hear him and to be healed of their diseases (6:17–19). In their presence, he commends to his disciples a life of love and non-judgmental generosity (6:20–42). Those who have received the mercy and forgiveness of God are to show similar grace in their relationship with others. This teaching segment concludes with a warning about what the heart produces (6:43–45), and a related challenge about hearing his words and putting them into practice (6:46–49).

Jesus' warning about fruit from the heart is 'a call to a true inner goodness of the heart, of which one's concrete acts of goodness will be the natural fruit'.[20] This parallels John the Baptist's demand for the fruit of genuine repentance (3:7–14). Jesus demonstrates a perception of what is going on in human hearts (5:22; 9:47; 24:25, 38), and warns about the devil taking away the word of God from

---

19. Cf. R. C. Tannehill, 'Repentance in the Context of Lukan Soteriology', in *The Shape of Luke's Story: Essays on Luke-Acts* (Eugene: Cascade, 2005), pp. 84–101.

20. Nolland, *Luke 1–9:20*, p. 309. In the immediate context, Jesus 'cuts through the hypocrisy, shallowness, and self-deceit of every paraded goodness of externality'.

the heart, 'so that they may not believe and be saved' (8:12). He particularly observes the way the heart can be corrupted by riches (12:34; 16:14–15), and 'weighed down with dissipation and drunkenness and cares of this life' (21:34; 12:45). However, those who hear the word and hold it fast in an honest and good heart 'bear fruit with patience' (8:15).

So the gospel Jesus preaches can transform hearts and produce the fruit God requires. Even though he does not explicitly talk about the law being written on the heart, Jesus links spiritual and ethical renewal with belief in his message about forgiveness. In this respect, the echo of Jeremiah 31:31–34 is clear.

Redemption accomplished

In Leviticus 25, Jubilee liberation is to be proclaimed every fiftieth year on the Day of Atonement.[21] In Isaiah 58:6; 61:1–2 the terminology is applied to a definitive release of Israel from everything hindering her relationship with God and ability to do his will. This implies a new act of redemption for God's people, surpassing the exodus from Egypt and the covenantal provisions that ensued. Luke's account of Jesus' programmatic sermon in 4:16–30, together with his wider use of the expression 'the forgiveness of sins' suggests that Isaiah's promise of a Jubilee-type liberation for Israel is fulfilled through a new form of atonement. Luke's concluding chapters associate this with the death of Jesus.

---

21. The Jubilee laws in Lev. 25 are grounded on the exodus event and Israel's status as a people saved by God to be his servants. As well as regulations concerning the release of land, the Jubilee laws provide for the release of slaves and the care of the destitute and needy. Deut. 15 deals with the closely related instructions for release (*aphesis*) every seventh year. In Isaiah's presentation, Israel in exile has become the debt slave who has lost its land and requires release, return and restoration.

The Last Supper sayings

There is much anticipation of Jesus' death in Luke's Gospel, particularly as he foretells the circumstances and teaches about the implications for his disciples (9:18–27, 31, 43–45, 51–62; 13:31–34; 18:31–34). But nothing is said about its atoning significance until Jesus addresses the disciples in the upper room. Many scholars have argued that Luke sees no soteriological significance in the crucifixion and that he does not connect it with the forgiveness of sins.[22] However, Jesus' words in connection with the cup at the Last Supper speak of his death inaugurating the New Covenant (22:20) and clearly link this to the shedding of his blood ('the new covenant in my blood').[23] Contextually, this is associated with the fulfilment of the Passover 'in the kingdom of God' (22:15–18).

The Passover was an annual celebration of Israel's redemption from Egypt (Exod. 12 – 13). With this redemption came the establishment of the covenant that was sealed with sacrificial blood (Exod. 19 – 24). But with the death of Jesus an even greater act of redemption is accomplished, and 'from now on it is to the covenant sealed in the blood of Jesus that believers look as they anticipate the future coming of the kingdom of God'.[24] The Passover is fulfilled in the sacrificial death of Jesus, which makes participation in the eschatological banquet of the kingdom of God possible.

In Mark 14:24 Jesus says, 'This is *my* blood of the covenant, which is poured out for many', alluding to Exodus 24:8 ('the blood of the covenant'), but making the newness of the situation clear with

22. H. Conzelmann, *The Theology of St. Luke*, tr. G. Buswell (New York: Harper & Row, 1960), pp. 200–201, was influential in the development of this approach. D. D. Sylva (ed.), *Reimaging the Death of the Lukan Jesus* (Frankfurt: Anton Hain, 1990), offers a number of alternative views.

23. J. B. Green, 'The Death of Jesus, God's Servant', in Sylva, *Reimaging*, pp. 3–4. The absence of 22:19b–20 from part of the Western textual tradition leaves some scholars in doubt about the originality of this reading, but the longer reading is widely attested and is included in the best ancient manuscripts. Cf. B. M. Metzger (ed.), *A Textual Commentary on the Greek New Testament*, 2nd ed. (Stuttgart: Deutsche Bibelgesellschaft, 1994), pp. 148–150.

24. J. Nolland, *Luke 18:35 – 24:53*, WBC 35C, p. 1044.

the preposition 'my'. Matthew 26:28 adds a more explicit reference
to Jeremiah 31:34 with the words 'This is my blood of the covenant,
which is poured out for many *for the forgiveness of sins*'. Luke 22:20 has
'the new covenant' instead of 'the forgiveness of sins', and a different
form of the saying similar to the tradition that Paul records: 'This
cup is the new covenant in my blood' (cf. 1 Cor. 11:25).[25]

Jesus goes on to declare that the Son of Man proceeds to his
death 'as it has been determined' (22:22), but only in Luke's account
does he explain the divine plan with a quotation from Isaiah 53. This
is introduced with the claim that 'this Scripture must be fulfilled
in me', and is followed by the affirmation 'for what is written about
me has its fulfilment' (22:37). The reference itself, that he 'was
numbered with the transgressors' (Isa. 53:12), could simply relate to
his crucifixion between two criminals. However, it is more likely
from the way Luke's passion narrative unfolds that the whole of
Isaiah 53 is in view.[26] Indeed, the phrase '[he] was numbered with
the transgressors' shows that Jesus was 'occupied with the fact that
he, who least deserved it, was to be punished as a wrongdoer'.[27]

Crucifixion, resurrection and commissioning

Luke demonstrates the fulfilment of Isaiah 53 in his detailed account
of Jesus' crucifixion between two criminals (23:32–33, 39–43) by

---

25. Nolland, ibid., pp. 1042–1047, discusses the relationship between these
    different forms of the cup word and scholarly attempts to discern the
    original saying. Nolland, p. 1054, observes that 'despite the grammar, it
    must be the blood and not the cup that is poured out'. Susanne Lehne,
    The New Covenant in Hebrews, JSNTSS 44 (Sheffield: JSOT Press, 1990),
    pp. 80–85, argues that the two strands of Last Supper tradition (Mark/
    Matthew and Luke/Paul) 'concur in associating the motifs of death, blood,
    expiation and covenant'.
26. Cf. Green, 'Death of Jesus', pp. 22–23. W. J. Larkin Jr., 'Luke's Use of the
    Old Testament', *JETS* 20.4 (1977), pp. 326–336, provides a detailed treatment
    of the way Luke's Passion narrative reflects the fulfilment of Isa. 53.
27. R. T. France, *Jesus and the Old Testament* (London: Tyndale, 1971), p. 115. So
    the penal substitutionary death of the Servant outlined in Isa. 53 as a whole
    is suggested by this particular verse.

the way in which the Roman centurion declares the innocence of Jesus (23:47), and by Jesus' prayer from the cross 'Father, forgive them, for they know not what they do' (23:34).[28] This expresses his earnest desire that even those who betrayed him should benefit from the fruit of his suffering (cf. Isa. 53:10–12). When one of the criminals asks Jesus to remember him when he comes into his kingdom, Jesus responds, 'Truly, I say to you, today you will be with me in Paradise' (23:43). Confident that God will raise him from death, he assures those who believe in him of a share with him in the promised New Creation.

When he is raised, Jesus explains the scriptural necessity for his suffering and resurrection to the disciples (24:26, 44–46). On that basis he indicates that repentance and forgiveness of sins should be proclaimed in his name 'to all nations, beginning from Jerusalem' (24:47). This form of words is unique to Luke's Gospel. Its universal scope reflects the expectation of passages like Isaiah 40:5, 49:5–6, but also Jeremiah's predictions about the national and international implications of the promised salvation (Jer. 3:17; 12:16; 16:19–21; 33:9). Jesus' commission emphasizes that repentance and the forgiveness of sins are the fruit of his redemptive work. *These gifts of God for the restoration of Israel and the salvation of the nations are to be proclaimed as part of the apostolic gospel* (cf. Acts 2:38; 5:31; 13:38–39; 20:21).

Conclusions so far

Although the Third Gospel is much influenced by Isaiah's predictions about the future of Israel, the promise of a new covenant in Jeremiah 31:31–34 is critical for Luke's presentation of the

---

28. Luke 23:34a is not found in some of the best manuscripts (cf. Metzger, *Textual Commentary*, p. 154). Nolland, *Luke 18:35 – 24:53*, p. 1144, argues that the prayer from the cross has 'good claim to being based upon historical reminiscence'. It is also worth noting with Marshall, *Luke*, p. 868, that 'sayings by Jesus are found in each main section of the Lucan crucifixion narrative (23:28–31, 43, 46); the lack of such a saying at this point would disturb the pattern'.

redemptive work of Jesus.[29] This is so because of the climactic allusion in 22:20 and because of the way Luke relates the forgiveness of sins to the saving plan of God at various points throughout his first volume, especially in 1:77 and 24:46–47.

Luke does not explicitly contrast the New Covenant with the Mosaic or Sinai Covenant, but implies that it is the fulfilment of the covenant made with Abraham and the fathers of Israel (Luke 1:73–75; cf. Acts 3:25; 7:8). Nevertheless, he clearly shows that the blessings of the New Covenant are based on the saving work of Christ, rather than on the exodus redemption or the atoning provisions of the law. Furthermore,

> a case can be made that Luke thinks Jesus' proclamation of God's reign (with its associated ethical teaching) and the presence of the Spirit in Israel have effectively displaced the Law from its central position in the relationship between God and his people.[30]

A transformative, rather than a purely forensic, view of forgiveness is implied by several passages in Luke's Gospel (3:3–14; 5:17–26, 27–32; 7:36–50; cf. 19:1–10). Release can be experienced from sin's power, as well as from its penalty. The forgiveness Jesus offers is an incentive for repentance and love. Since transformation in the prophetic writings is also related to the work of the Holy Spirit, we now turn to consider the fulfilment of that hope in Acts.

---

29. Jer. 31:34 LXX (*hileōs esomai tais adikiais autōn kai tōn hamartiōn autōn ou mē mnēsthō eti*) may not be directly responsible for the terminology that is regularly used in Luke-Acts for the forgiveness of sins (*aphesis hamartiōn* or various forms of the verb *aphiēmi* with reference to sins). Isa. 33:24, 55:7 uses the terminology familiar to us from Luke-Acts, but a range of different expressions convey the same hope in other contexts (e.g. 1:18; 40:2). Isa. 61:1–2, 58:6, with proclamations of a Jubilee 'release' (*aphesis*), appear to have been influential for both Jesus and Luke in this connection.

30. Turner, *Power*, p. 354.

Redemption applied

Acts 1:1–14 looks back in summary fashion to the concluding scenes of Luke's Gospel and prepares for the great events soon to be narrated. The command to wait in Jerusalem for the promised Spirit is repeated, but expanded to include a version of John the Baptist's prediction (Acts 1:4–5; cf. Luke 24:49).[31] Jesus' commissioning of his witnesses is then expressed in terms of the geographical progress by which their testimony will extend from Jerusalem, Judea and Samaria 'to the end of the earth' (1:8; cf. Luke 24:46–48). The ascension and its immediate outcome are also more fully described than at the end of the Gospel (1:9–14; cf. Luke 24:50–53).

Israel and the kingdom of God

Most significant for our purpose is the question of the apostles 'Lord, will you at this time restore the kingdom to Israel?' (1:6). Jesus does not rebuke them for their question,[32] but clearly indicates that 'it is not for you to know times or seasons that the Father has fixed by his own authority' (1:7). He goes on to speak about the gift of the Spirit and the fulfilment of prophecies about Israel as a servant community, called to be God's 'witnesses' to the nations (1:8; cf. Isa. 43:10, 12; 44:8). The end-time restoration begins with the pouring out of the promised Spirit and the bringing of God's salvation, first to Israel and then 'to the ends of the earth' (Isa. 49:6; 42:6–7). It is consummated when Jesus returns (Acts 1:11; 3:20–21). Through the witness of Jesus' apostles, 'the kingdom' is restored to Israel, but

---

31. Dunn, *Baptism*, p. 43, suggests that this modification of the Baptist's prediction reflects the fact that Jesus, as Servant of the Lord, suffers on behalf of his people: 'the fire is kindled on him; he is baptized with the messianic baptism of others; he drains the cup of wrath which was the portion of others'. Cf. Turner, *Power*, pp. 186–187.

32. Cf. R. C. Tannehill, *The Narrative Unity of Luke-Acts: A Literary Interpretation.* Vol. 2: *The Acts of the Apostles* (Minneapolis: Fortress, 1990), pp. 14–17; Pao, *Acts*, pp. 95–96.

not in nationalistic or political terms, nor immediately in the full and final sense outlined in biblical prophecy (cf. 3:19–26).

The validity of this interpretation is demonstrated by the following narratives. A twelfth apostle is first chosen to be an authorized witness to the people (1:21–26; cf. 5:32; 13:31). This is in line with Jesus' declaration that twelve would share in his rule and 'sit on thrones judging the twelve tribes of Israel' (Luke 22:30; cf. Matt. 19:28). The Spirit is then poured out on the apostles and about 120 others who are prayerfully anticipating this gift (1:12–15; 2:1–4). Luke's description of the crowd on that Day of Pentecost (2:5–11) indicates that this critical event took place in the presence of Jews and proselytes from many nations: 'just as the Twelve represent the nucleus of the people that is being restored, so does this audience represent all the lands to which the Jews had been dispersed'.[33]

Peter's Pentecost proclamation points to the fulfilment of Joel's prophecy about the renewal of Israel through the outpouring of his Spirit (Acts 2:14–21; cf. Joel. 2:28–32). This is a sign that 'the day of the Lord' is near, and so it is time to call upon 'the name of the Lord', to be saved from the approaching judgment. But the rest of Peter's message shows that *Jesus* is the Lord upon whom they must now call (2:22–36). Although Jesus was killed 'by the hands of lawless men', God raised him from death in fulfilment of Psalm 16:8–11. Exalted to the right hand of God in fulfilment of Psalm 110:1, he has received from the Father the promised Holy Spirit, whom he has poured out for all to see and hear. Peter's climactic challenge to 'all the house of Israel' is that they should know for certain that 'God has made him both Lord and Christ, this Jesus whom you crucified'.

The Messiah's rule is from heaven and the renewal of Israel begins with the preaching of the gospel about Jesus and his pouring

---

33. L. T. Johnson, *The Acts of the Apostles*, SP 5 (Collegeville: Liturgical, 1992), p. 47. I. H. Marshall, 'The Significance of Pentecost', *SJT* 30 (1977), p. 357, rightly observes that 'if the description of Pentecost is meant to foreshadow the world-wide expansion of the church, it is an expansion among *Jews* scattered throughout the world that is used to provide the picture'.

out of the Spirit.[34] When Peter's audience is 'cut to the heart' and ask what they should do, the reply comes back,

> Repent and be baptized every one of you in the name of Jesus Christ for the forgiveness of your sins, and you will receive the gift of the Holy Spirit. For the promise is for you and for your children and for all who are far off, everyone whom the Lord our God calls to himself. (2:38–39)

In the progress of Luke's narrative, this is a very significant passage. As commanded in Luke 24:47, Jesus' followers offer forgiveness and call their fellow Israelites to repent *in his name*. Repentance is a human responsibility, but it is the gift of God, made possible by his promise of forgiveness (cf. 3:26; 5:31; 11:18).

The Spirit and salvation

In the post-Pentecost situation, the gift of the Spirit is linked with the offer of salvation (2:40), and baptism 'in the name of Jesus Christ' is the means of expressing repentance and receiving by faith the benefits promised.[35] Water baptism is closely connected with the bestowal of the Spirit in 2:38–39, but the link cannot be pressed too strongly since the gift of the Spirit sometimes precedes and sometimes follows baptism in other contexts (cf. 8:12, 14–17; 9:17–18; 10:44–48; 19:5–6).[36]

---

34. Cf. A. J. Thompson, *The Acts of the Risen Lord Jesus: Luke's Account of God's Unfolding Plan*, NSBT 27 (Nottingham: Apollos; Downers Grove: InterVarsity Press Academic, 2011).

35. The 'name' of Jesus represents his divine authority and power to grant the blessing of the Spirit and to save people from the coming judgment through the forgiveness of sins (cf. Joel 2:32; Acts 4:12; 5:31; 10:43; 13:38). At the human level, calling upon Jesus as Lord and Messiah is essentially what makes a person a Christian (2:36; cf. Rom. 10:9–10).

36. The expression 'gift of the Holy Spirit' recalls Jesus' promise to those who pray (Luke 11:13; cf. Acts 8:20; 10:45; 11:17). Christian baptism can be regarded as a means of prayer to God for the gift of his Spirit. But note that the gift consists of the Spirit himself and that this gift is to be distinguished from the gifts that the Spirit imparts (cf. 1 Cor. 12:7–11).

The Spirit in Acts is not simply given to equip believers for service but to make possible the sort of transformed relationship with God promised in passages such as Isaiah 32:15–17; 44:2–5; Ezekiel 11:19–20; 36:26–27.[37] Although Jeremiah 31:31–34 does not mention the Spirit's work, the prophet indicates that God will put his law within them and write it on their heart, so that they will *all* know him 'from the least of them to the greatest' (cf. Jer. 24:7). In the teaching of Jesus and the apostles, these prophetic expectations are viewed as being fulfilled in the same salvific events. Joel 2:28–32 also speaks about the restoration of Israel in different, but related, terms. When one of these passages is quoted or alluded to in the New Testament, the whole pattern of prophetic expectation seems to be in view. Theologically these promises belong together, since spiritual renewal cannot take place without forgiveness and repentance being experienced, and this means coming to know the Lord as he has revealed himself in Jesus the Messiah (cf. Acts 3:13–26; 4:9–12; 10:24–43; 13:38–39).

The covenantal aspect of this renewal is suggested by the words 'for you and for your children and for all who are far off, everyone whom the Lord our God calls to himself'. *The promise* is most obviously the promise of the Spirit about which Jesus spoke during his earthly ministry (Luke 24:49; Acts 1:4). More generally, however, God's promise in Acts means his covenant commitment to Abraham and the patriarchs of Israel (3:25; 7:17; 26:6). This finds its consummation in the sending of the Messiah (13:23, 32), who pours out the promised Holy Spirit on his disciples (2:33). Luke seems to share Paul's equation of 'the blessing of Abraham' with the gift of the Spirit (Gal. 3:14). 'Implicit here, therefore, is the thought of the Spirit as the new covenant fulfillment of the ancient covenant promise.'[38]

---

37. Turner, *Power*, pp. 352–360, rightly argues against the view that the Spirit is simply a *donum superadditum* – an additional gift for mission proclamation – and contends that the Spirit is given as an element of the salvation promised.

38. Dunn, *Baptism*, p. 47. Cf. C. K. Barrett, *A Critical and Exegetical Commentary on the Acts of the Apostles*, vol. 1, ICC (Edinburgh: T. & T. Clark, 1994), p. 155.

The expression 'for you and your children' develops Joel's promise of the Spirit being poured out 'on all flesh' (Joel 2:28–29). God's covenant mercies were for Peter's Jewish audience and for their descendants (cf. Gen. 13:15; 17:7–9; Acts 13:32–33). They were also for Jews scattered in other places (cf. Isa. 57:19; Jer. 3:17–18; 31:8–9; 50:4–5). Although those who are 'far off' could include the Gentiles, Luke's 'geographical approach to history writing and the telling of the story of the early church' makes a reference to 'Jews in distant lands' more likely at this point.[39] The final description of the people for whom the promise is made recalls the last clause of Joel 2:32 (not quoted in Acts 2:21). The blessings of salvation will be for 'everyone whom the Lord our God calls to himself'. People everywhere must call on the name of the Lord Jesus for deliverance, but *he* must first call *them* and enable them to respond to his gracious initiative.

When Peter says 'save yourselves from this crooked generation' (2:40), he picks up the language of Joel again, where salvation from the coming judgment of God is meant (cf. Acts 2:19–21).[40] But salvation from 'this crooked generation' points to the need for rescue from something more immediate. In order to escape from the final judgment of God, Peter's audience needed to be rescued from the corrupting and damning influence of their society. This recalls the charge of Jesus that his generation was unbelieving, perverse (Luke 7:31–35; 9:41) and wicked (11:29–32). They followed the trend of previous generations, who rejected God's messengers (11:50–52; 17:25) and effectively killed the one sent to them by God (Acts 2:22–23; cf. 3:13–15; 7:51–53).

Wider use of such terminology in Luke-Acts suggests that people in general need to be saved 'because they are part of one of the many generations that have failed or is presently failing before God

---

39. B. Witherington, *The Acts of the Apostles: A Socio-Rhetorical Commentary* (Grand Rapids: Eerdmans; Carlisle: Paternoster, 1998), pp. 155–156.

40. NKJV more accurately renders the Greek passive (*sōthēte*) 'be saved', which implies that salvation is the action of God in the lives of those who repent and believe.

and thus constitute corrupt humanity'.[41] Those who want to be
saved from the judgment of God need to distance themselves from
their generation and identify with Jesus and his cause. Peter's call to
his contemporaries implies that the disciples of Jesus are the nucleus
of a renewed Israel, to which they should attach themselves.

The Spirit's transforming work

Three thousand people repent and believe through the preaching
of Peter (2:41), forming a community that is united in praise of God
and service to one another, 'having favour with all the people' (2:42–
47).[42] The Spirit's involvement in this process is clarified when Luke
later speaks about the church throughout all Judea and Galilee and
Samaria growing in size and maturity, 'in the encouragement of the
Holy Spirit' (9:31, my tr.).

Luke's detailed portrait of the church in Jerusalem shows what
happened when Jews were bound together by a belief in the gospel,
an understanding of its implications and an enjoyment of its
blessings. In view of the promises in Jeremiah 24:7, 31:33 and
32:39–40, it is particularly interesting that Luke says the believers
were 'of one heart and soul' (4:32, *kardia kai psychē mia*). In practical
terms, this involved sharing food and possessions, as well as praying
and praising God together (cf. 2:44–47; 6:1–6; 11:27–30). Although
such unity and joyful sharing fulfilled certain ideals in the Hellenistic
world,[43] Luke is essentially concerned to demonstrate the fulfilment

41. C. Stenschke, 'The Need for Salvation', in I. H. Marshall and D. G. Peterson
    (eds.), *Witness to the Gospel: The Theology of Acts* (Grand Rapids: Eerdmans,
    1998), p. 140. Stenschke, pp. 135–140, reviews the use of 'generation'
    language in Luke-Acts and discusses OT parallels. Sin is treated as a
    universal problem in Acts, requiring salvation for Jews and Gentiles alike.
    Cf. Phil. 2:15; 1 Pet. 1:18–19.

42. In *The Acts of the Apostles*, PNTC (Grand Rapids: Eerdmans; Nottingham:
    Apollos, 2009), p. 164, I argue that the expression in 2:47 (*echontes charin pros
    holon ton laon*) could mean 'having goodwill towards all the people'.

43. Seccombe, *Possessions*, pp. 200–218; L. T. Johnson, *The Acts of the Apostles*,
    SP 5 (Collegeville: Liturgical, 1992), pp. 61–63.

of God's covenant promises to Israel concerning the renewal of his people.[44]

The restoration of all things

The apostles performed 'many signs and wonders ... among the people' (5:12; cf. 2:43; 4:30; 5:15–16), but the healing of a man crippled from birth in 3:1–10 is the only detailed account of such activity in Jerusalem. The narrative stresses the suddenness and completeness of the cure, together with the wonder and amazement of the bystanders. In the speech that follows, this miracle is attributed to the glorified Lord Jesus (3:11–26), whose identity is then proclaimed in terms of the fulfilment of various Scriptures. The audience is challenged to repent and turn to God for forgiveness, especially acknowledging their part in the death of Jesus.

Three positive encouragements to repent are given in a series of purpose clauses (3:19–20). The first is 'that your sins may be blotted out', using a graphic term that recalls the promise of Isaiah 43:25 ('I am he who blots out your transgressions for my own sake, / and I will not remember your sins'). This restates the offer of forgiveness proclaimed in 2:38, but the language emphasizes the erasure of sin and its ongoing consequences (cf. Jer. 31:34). The idea that this offer of forgiveness is new and decisive, having eschatological significance, is reinforced by the second purpose clause: 'that times of refreshing may come from the presence of the Lord'. No verbal parallels to this expression have been found in Scripture, but a comparison with Peter's promises in 2:38 suggests that the Holy Spirit is the one who brings this refreshment. Peter may be describing the subjective effect of the gift of the Spirit for believers, whose presence anticipates and guarantees the full inheritance God promises his children (cf. 2 Cor. 1:22; Eph. 1:14).[45]

---

44. Johnson, *Acts*, p. 91, suggests that Luke's manner of expression in Acts 2 and 4 is designed to show how the primitive community in Jerusalem realized 'the best ideals both of Hellenism and Judaism concerning life together'.

45. See alternative interpretations of this verse in Peterson, *Acts*, pp. 180–181.

The apostle finally urges the Jerusalem Jews to repent so that God may 'send the Christ appointed for you, Jesus, whom heaven must receive until the time for restoring all the things about which God spoke by the mouth of his holy prophets long ago' (Acts 3:20–21). Peter's point is that the previously rejected Messiah will return only if Israel repents. As he speaks of the Christ bringing about the promised restoration of all things (*apokatastaseōs pantōn*), it becomes clear that the physical healing of the lame man is a sign of the messianic salvation in all its dimensions. The restoration of Israel is part of this process (the cognate verb *apokathistēmi* is used in 1:6). However, the healing of the crippled man anticipates the ultimate renewal of the whole created order, associated with the coming of the Messiah (cf. Amos 9:11–15; Isa. 35:1–10; 65:17–25; Ezek. 47:1–12). Furthermore, Peter goes on to teach that the blessing of all peoples on earth through the messianic restoration of Israel must first take place (Acts 3:25–26). In other words, the restoration of all things has begun and will continue until it is consummated at Christ's return.

With the offer of this salvation comes also a warning about continuing to reject Jesus and thus being cut off from 'the people' (3:22–23). Peter refers to Deuteronomy 18:15, 19, where Moses says, 'The Lord God will raise up for you a prophet like me from your brothers.' This was in the context of warning Israel not to be like the nations. Instead of practising sorcery or divination, they were to 'listen to him in whatever he tells you'. The warning is then individualized with the addition of words from Leviticus 23:29, 'every soul who does not listen to that prophet shall be destroyed from the people'. In time, Moses' prophecy came to be regarded as messianic in its scope.[46] Peter envisages Jesus as that prophet, because he brings the ultimate revelation of God's will and leads God's people

---

46. For Jewish, Samaritan and Christian interpretations of this hope, see H. M. Teeple, *The Mosaic Eschatological Prophet*, JBLMS 10 (Philadelphia: JBL, 1957), pp. 63–68, 100–121. Jesus is hailed as 'the Prophet' in John 6:14, 7:40, and the divine command at his transfiguration ('listen to him', Mark 9:7 par.) echoes Deut. 18:15, suggesting that Jesus is the expected prophet.

to final salvation. Jesus functions for Israel as Moses did at the time of the exodus. By their response to the resurrected Jesus, Peter's audience show whether they belong to the true Israel or not!

Peter concludes his appeal by declaring that 'all the prophets who have spoken, from Samuel and those who came after him, also proclaimed these days' (3:24). In other words, there is a comprehensive revelation about the last days in the prophetic literature and it is all being fulfilled in the Lord Jesus and the ministry he has given to his agents. Peter continues, 'You are the sons of the prophets and of the covenant that God made with your fathers, saying to Abraham, "And in your offspring shall all the families of the earth be blessed"' (3:25; cf. Gen. 12:3; 22:18). By implication, they ought to be the beneficiaries of everything promised by the prophets concerning the messianic restoration of God's people. However, as heirs of the covenant made with Abraham, Isaac and Jacob, 'they do not have a right to the covenant itself irrespective of their reaction to Jesus'.[47] Peter once more indicates that repentance is necessary in response to God's saving grace: 'God, having raised up his servant, sent him to you first, to bless you by turning every one of you from your wickedness' (3:26).

Use of the word 'first' (*prōton*) implies the sort of sequence portrayed in Isaiah 49:5–6, where the Servant of the Lord is used to 'raise up the tribes of Jacob' so that they can be 'a light for the nations' and bring God's salvation 'to the end of the earth' (cf. Acts 1:6; 13:46–48; 26:16–18). In other words, Isaiah's vision of the way in which God will ultimately fulfil his promise to Abraham appears to lie behind the final challenge of Peter's sermon.[48] At this point in the narrative Peter clearly anticipates that the messianic salvation will somehow be extended to the nations. In Acts 10 – 11 he is faced with more precise questions: How might Gentiles actually receive

---

47. Barrett, *Acts*, vol. 1, p. 212.
48. Barrett, ibid., p. 213, argues that in this sequence of thought the raising up of Jesus more naturally refers to God sending him as his Servant, to accomplish his plan for Israel and the nations, rather than to his resurrection.

the gospel from believing Jews and be united with them in the community of the Messiah?

To the nations

The positive result of Peter's proclamation in Acts 3 is that many more are added to the number of the disciples (4:4). But the incident also initiates a process of opposition, leading to the death of Stephen and the scattering of the church from Jerusalem through persecution. The gospel is proclaimed in Samaria and beyond, leading eventually to the incorporation of many Gentiles into the fellowship of believers (Acts 8 – 14). Using the testimony of believing Israelites, the Spirit progressively brings people from many races and religious backgrounds to share in the New Covenant blessings.

Luke mentions the forgiveness of sins at key points in the rest of the narrative. The first is Peter's encounter with Cornelius and his household in Caesarea. As a 'God-fearer' (10:1–2) Cornelius appears to have been a Gentile synagogue member, but not yet a full convert to Judaism. He is a bridge figure, 'standing at the boundary between Judaism and paganism, and living in a very Hellenized city full of Gentiles, yet in the Holy Land'.[49] Peter announces that Jesus is the one appointed by God to be the judge of the living and the dead and concludes, 'to him all the prophets bear witness that everyone who believes in him receives forgiveness of sins through his name' (10:42–43). Apart from 17:31 this is the most explicit statement in Acts about Jesus' role as universal judge, though it is implied in 2:34; 3:23; 7:56. The coming judgment is the context in which to understand the need for forgiveness 'through his name'. The combined witness of the prophets indicates that Jesus is the one who makes acquittal possible for 'everyone who believes in him', in advance of that final day.

For the first time Peter proclaims that the messianic salvation can be enjoyed by believers from every nation. As he speaks, the

---

49. Witherington, *Acts*, p. 340, n. 46. Cf. Peterson, *Acts*, pp. 326–327, on the status of Cornelius as a 'God-fearer'.

Spirit falls on those who hear the message, convincing Peter and his Jewish companions that Gentiles can belong to the renewed people of God without having to be circumcised or keep the law of Moses (10:44–48; 11:1–18). Later, at the Jerusalem Council, Peter reflects on this incident and declares that God 'made no distinction between us and them, having cleansed their hearts by faith' (15:9). Gentiles, who were previously unclean in Jewish eyes because they lacked the purifying benefits of the law, have been definitively cleansed because God enabled them to believe the gospel.[50]

In Luke's presentation of Paul's missionary preaching, the sermon in the synagogue at Pisidian Antioch gives the fullest version of his appeal to Jewish audiences. Although there are significant parallels with Peter's Pentecost speech, Paul begins with God's election of Israel to be his people and his choice of David to be their king (13:17–23). He then claims that because Jesus fulfils God's promises to David, he is the key to Israel's future (13:24–37). Indeed,

> the present episode underscores the conviction that Jesus' death and resurrection mark the 'necessary' (13:46) fulfilment of Israel's *entire* scriptural canon – 'the law and the prophets' (13:15, 27, 39–40) together with the psalms (13:33, 35).[51]

The climax of Paul's appeal is the claim that 'through this man forgiveness of sins is proclaimed to you, and by him everyone who believes is freed from everything from which you could not be freed by the law of Moses' (13:38–39). A Jewish audience might well have wondered why they needed such forgiveness, but John the Baptist's preaching had made it clear that all the people of Israel needed to engage in radical repentance, to be ready to meet their God (13:24).

---

50. Even though Cornelius had a genuine faith in God before he heard Peter's message (10:2–4, 22, 31), his faith became explicitly focused on Jesus as the promised saviour so that he and his companions were baptized 'in the name of Jesus Christ' (10:48).

51. F. S. Spencer, *Acts* (Sheffield: Sheffield Academic, 1997), p. 143 (original emphasis). Cf. Luke 24:44–45.

Furthermore, the prophets had promised that God would provide forgiveness and cleansing as part of the renewal of Israel in the last days.

The Greek text of Acts 13:39 could be translated, 'everyone who believes is justified' (*pas ho pisteuōn dikaioutai*), paralleling the argument of some of Paul's letters (e.g. Gal. 2:16; 3:11, 24).[52] However, the related expression *dikaiōthēnai apo* is best translated 'freed from' (ESV) or 'set free from' (NRSV, TNIV; cf. Rom. 6:7). Forgiveness sets people free from serving sin, so that they can offer themselves to God as 'instruments for righteousness' (cf. Rom. 6:11–14).

In Acts 13:38–39 Paul proclaims that faith in Jesus Christ sets people free from all those things from which it was impossible to find release in or by the law of Moses.[53] This suggests the ineffectiveness of the law to achieve a satisfactory atonement for sins and the sort of moral and spiritual transformation required by God. Forgiveness and renewal are now available for 'everyone who believes' in the gospel about Jesus and seeks these benefits 'through him' (13:38, *dia toutou*). Although Jeremiah 31:31–34 is not mentioned, the substance of that oracle is offered in terms of a decisive solution

---

52. Paul mostly uses the language of justification in a forensic sense, making it clear from Rom. 4:5–7 that this involves a non-imputation of sin and a positive reckoning of righteousness to the ungodly because of Christ's atoning work (cf. Rom. 3:21–26). In the same passage Paul shows the close relation between forgiveness and justification by citing Ps. 32:1. C. L. Blomberg, 'The Christian and the Law of Moses', in Marshall and Peterson, *Witness to the Gospel*, p. 406, rightly describes Acts 13:38–39 as 'actually one of the most Pauline statements in the entire book'.

53. The preposition *en* can be taken here in a locative sense, meaning 'in (the area marked out by the law)', or instrumentally, meaning 'by (obedience to the law)'. Paul expounds the weakness of the law to achieve justification and transformation of life in passages such as Rom. 3:19–20, 27–31; 7:1–6; 8:1–4. Witherington, *Acts*, pp. 413–414, argues that Acts 13:38 could mean 'that the Law of Moses was capable of setting things right in some matters, but that Jesus could provide justification in all cases'. However, this misses the epoch-changing implications of the sermon and the definitive and comprehensive nature of the forgiveness offered through Christ. Cf. Blomberg, 'Law', p. 406.

to the problem of sin, enabling God's people to serve him faithfully from the heart.

Later in Ephesus Paul recalls the ministry he had in that city, 'testifying both to Jews and to Greeks of repentance toward God and of faith in our Lord Jesus Christ' (20:21). He goes on to speak of the atoning work of Jesus for the church of God, 'which he obtained with his own blood' (20:28).[54] Then he commends his Jewish and Gentile converts 'to the word of his grace, which is able to build you up and give you the inheritance among all those who are sanctified' (20:32; cf. 26:18). Once again, the covenantal implications of the saving work of Jesus are proclaimed, only this time the incorporation of believing Gentiles in the blessings is made clear.

There is an interesting parallel between Luke's record of the Last Supper, where Jesus declared that the New Covenant would be inaugurated by the shedding of his blood (Luke 22:20), and Paul's teaching in Acts 20. The 'message of his grace', which proclaims the benefits of Christ's atoning death and his glorious exaltation, forms and sustains the church as the eschatological people of God. Ultimately, it enables his sanctified people to share together in the promised eternal inheritance.

A final mention of forgiveness occurs in Paul's defence speech before Herod Agrippa II and Festus the Roman governor. Recalling his appointment by the risen Lord Jesus to be a servant and witness, Paul mentions that he was sent both to his own people and to the Gentiles, 'to open their eyes, so that they may turn from darkness to light and from the power of Satan to God, that they may receive forgiveness of sins and a place among those who are sanctified by

---

54. Such covenantal language suggests that the Ephesian church belonged to God as his personal possession, having been *bought* (*periepoiēsato*) or acquired at a great price (cf. Exod. 19:5 [*laos periousios*]; Isa. 31:5; 43:21). Although many commentators seek to avoid the implication that Christ's death is the price paid for redeeming his people, the verb *peripoieomai* in combination with the expression *dia tou haimatos tou idiou*, surely means 'acquired with his own blood' or 'acquired with the blood of his own [Son]'. Cf. Peterson, *Acts*, pp. 569–570.

faith in me' (26:18). The language here suggests 'the continuity of Paul's mission with the scriptural prophets but also with the mission of Jesus announced in the Nazareth synagogue'.[55]

The risen Lord has used Paul to proclaim light both to Jews and Gentiles (26:23; cf. Col. 1:12–14; 2 Cor. 4:1–6). This has made it possible for individuals to turn from the power of Satan to God (13:6–12; 16:16–18; 19:13–20). Turning is closely linked to repentance in 26:20, both terms describing a regular aspect of Paul's preaching (14:15; 17:30; 20:21; 26:20; cf. 1 Thess. 1:9–10). Spiritual enlightenment and liberation from Satan's dominion require a turning away from other sources of illumination and control to seek a genuine relationship with God. Such a relationship involves the forgiveness of sins and sanctification in a covenantal and corporate sense. The ultimate outcome is a share with Christ in the resurrection from the dead (26:23).

Conclusion

In Luke-Acts, the forgiveness of sins is proclaimed by John the Baptist, Jesus, Peter and Paul. It is central to the 'release' that Jesus offers (Luke 4:18), which is a way of speaking about the redemption he makes possible. The covenantal dimensions of this redemption are revealed in various ways. A call for repentance is a challenge to return to the Lord of the covenant and to walk in his way. Repentance is regularly associated with the offer of forgiveness, empowering those who respond to live a new life of obedience and service to God. Atonement for sin through the death of Jesus, rather than through the provisions of the law, is implied in several contexts (Luke 22:20; Acts 13:38–39; 20:28). Jesus makes possible the restoration of Israel in her relationship with God, so that believing Israelites can proclaim repentance and forgiveness of sins in his name to all nations. In this way the original covenant promises made

---

55. Tannehill, *Acts*, p. 323.

by God to Abraham are fulfilled as the New Covenant is inaugurated and its benefits are shared with Gentiles.

Following the example of Jesus, Luke and the early Christian preachers blend together prophetic expectations regarding the messianic salvation and its covenantal implications. So, while the influence of Jeremiah 31:31–34 on their thinking can be traced, other texts are employed to fill out the picture. In particular, predictions about the need for the Spirit of God to transform lives and make gospel ministry possible are highlighted. When the teaching of the prophets is considered together, the eschatological gift of the Spirit is shown to be the means by which Jeremiah's promise about the law being written on the heart, so that each can know the Lord, is fulfilled.

Pastorally, the teaching of Luke-Acts in this connection has several important implications. First, the link between forgiveness and repentance is a warning against any presumption of cheap grace. As Paul puts it in Romans 2:4, 'God's kindness is meant to lead you to repentance'.

Secondly, those who receive the forgiveness of sins made possible by the atoning death of Jesus, together with the gift of his Spirit, are empowered to live new lives to his glory. Hearts are changed through coming to know the grace of God in the person and work of Jesus. This is the transforming knowledge of God that Jeremiah predicted. Such transformation is relational and moral. Devotion to Jesus, rather than to the law of Moses, is the key.

Thirdly, God who has been faithful in fulfilling his covenant promises can be trusted to continue transforming lives through the preaching of the gospel and the enabling of his Spirit. Acts shows that evangelism and the nurture of believers are divine activities, accomplished through human agents, to achieve God's covenant plan for the blessing of the nations. Those who engage in these ministries today can share the confidence of the apostles in God's enabling.

Fourthly, forgiveness though Jesus anticipates the acquittal of final judgment, while the gift of the Holy Spirit anticipates the resurrection life of God's kingdom. These eschatological gifts are the solid basis for hope in a world where temptation, sin, persecution, sickness and death continue to assault believers and cause doubt.

Fifthly, the renewal provided by the New Covenant is not for individuals in isolation but for God's people collectively. Restored Israel becomes the nucleus of the church, which in due course includes people from every nation. The gospel of grace, in the power of the Spirit, nurtures and transforms believing communities, giving them one heart and mind and enabling God's light to shine through them into a dark world.

3. THE RENEWAL OF WORSHIP

Jeremiah's prophecy of a new covenant features more prominently in Hebrews than in any other New Testament document. It is quoted in full as the writer begins to explain how the high-priestly ministry of Jesus fulfils and replaces the provisions of the Mosaic Covenant (Heb. 8:8–12). An abbreviated version of the oracle then concludes the central doctrinal section (10:15–18), before the writer turns to application and exhortation. The New Covenant is also mentioned by name in 9:15 and 12:24. Elsewhere, it is called 'a better covenant' (7:22; 8:6) and 'the eternal covenant' (13:20).[1]

As in previous sections of Hebrews, a key biblical text is foundational to the argument in chapters 8–10, with other scriptures

---

1. The word 'covenant' (*diathēkē*) actually occurs seventeen times in Hebrews, with reference to both dispensations. But six times in the Greek text the noun is understood (8:7 [twice]; 8:13 [twice]; 9:1, 18), making a total of twenty-three. Susanne Lehne, *The New Covenant in Hebrews*, JSNTSS 44 (Sheffield: JSOT Press, 1990), pp. 11–12, also notices 'scattered echoes of covenantal language and thought patterns' (e.g. 6:7–8; 12:18–28).

being drawn into the exposition.[2] The full quotation from Jeremiah
31:31–34, which mostly follows the Septuagint (LXX 38:31–34), is
the longest single citation in the New Testament. Additionally,
Exodus 25:40 is quoted in 8:5, Exodus 24:8 in 9:20, and Psalm 40:6–8
in 10:5–10. There are also allusions to many other biblical texts in
the development of this section.

Before Jeremiah's oracle is cited, Hebrews establishes that the
ministry of Jesus is superior to that of the priesthood instituted by
Moses under the Sinai Covenant. First, as the crucified, resurrected
and ascended Son of God, he is a priest *for ever* (7:15–17; cf. Ps.
110:4), and 'always lives to make intercession' for his people (7:25).
Secondly, as the messianic high priest who is 'seated at the right hand
of the throne of the Majesty in heaven', he serves in the *heavenly*
sanctuary, 'in the true tent that the Lord set up, not man' (8:1–2; cf.
Ps. 110:1; Exod. 25:40). As such, he is the mediator and guarantor
of a 'better covenant' (7:22). The ministry he has received is superior
to that of the Levitical priests and the covenant he mediates is better,
since it is said to be 'enacted on better promises' (8:6).

Several things are unusual about the use of Jeremiah's prophecy
in Hebrews. First, the writer proclaims that the New Covenant is
inaugurated by the sacrifice of Jesus and his heavenly exaltation,
whereas the prophet gives no indication of the way the promised
forgiveness of sins is to be achieved.[3] Secondly, the New Covenant

---

2. Ps. 8:4–6 is foundational in 2:5–18, Ps. 95:7–11 in 3:7 – 4:13, and Ps. 110:4
   in 5:1 – 7:28. Cf. R. N. Longenecker, *Biblical Exegesis in the Apostolic Period*
   (Grand Rapids: Eerdmans, 1975), pp. 158–185; D. G. Peterson, 'God and
   Scripture in Hebrews', in P. Helm and C. Trueman (eds.), *The Trustworthiness*
   of God: Perspectives on the Nature of Scripture (Leicester: Apollos; Grand
   Rapids: Eerdmans, 2002), pp. 118–138.

3. It is highly likely that Hebrews was influenced by the saying of Jesus at the
   Last Supper, which formed part of the tradition passed on by the apostle
   Paul and no doubt other early Christian missionaries as well (1 Cor.
   11:23–25; cf. Luke 22:20). However, the novel contribution of Hebrews is
   to view the heavenly exaltation of Jesus as the means by which his sacrifice
   becomes perpetually available to all who draw near to God through him.
   Cf. Lehne, *New Covenant*, pp. 86–87.

brings a new way of approaching God, fulfilling and replacing the system established under the Old Covenant. Jeremiah only hints at this (Jer. 3:16–18), as other prophets do in their own distinctive ways (e.g. Isa. 2:1–4; Mal. 3:1–12). Thirdly, the promise of the law being put in the mind of God's people and written on their heart appears to be fulfilled in the renewed worship of the people of God. Worship clearly has an ethical, whole-of-life dimension in Hebrews (9:14; 12:28 – 13:16), which is consistent with Jeremiah's predictions about transformed attitudes and behaviour. Fourthly, the New Covenant makes it possible for those who are called to receive 'the promised eternal inheritance' (9:15). Jeremiah's hope for the restoration of his people is focused on their return to the Promised Land. Hebrews picks up the eschatological and heavenly application of this theme found in the teaching of Jesus and early Christian writings and links it to the establishment of the New Covenant.

The mediator

When the 'better covenant' is first mentioned in Hebrews, Jesus is described as its 'guarantor' or 'surety' (7:22). The legal term *engyos* appears only here in the New Testament, but it was commonly used in Hellenistic Greek to describe someone who assumed responsibility for another person's debt.[4] God's oath, confirming the eternity of Jesus' priesthood in Psalm 110:4, stands behind the writer's claim (7:20–21). The word proclaimed about this priesthood is fulfilled in the death and heavenly exaltation of the Messiah, making him 'a pledge of the new covenant, guaranteeing its eternal effectiveness'.[5]

The concepts of 'mediator' (8:6; 9:15; 12:24) and 'guarantor' are related but not identical. The legal term *mesitēs* was widely used of any sort of arbiter or intermediary, especially in disputes. However,

4. Cf. Sirach 29.14–19; Prov. 17:18; 22:26; H. Preisker, *TDNT* 2:329.
5. P. T. O'Brien, *The Letter to the Hebrews*, PNTC (Grand Rapids: Eerdmans; Nottingham: Apollos, 2010), pp. 271–272.

since the New Covenant is a gracious gift from God and not an agreement hammered out between God and his people, Jesus acts as mediator when he sheds his blood to inaugurate this covenant and makes its benefits available.[6]

Hebrews closely links his role as 'mediator of a new covenant' with his death that redeems believers from 'transgressions committed under the first covenant' (9:15).[7] His sacrifice retrospectively benefits those who otherwise would have failed to receive 'the promised eternal inheritance'. But God also 'brought again from the dead our Lord Jesus, the great shepherd of the sheep, by the blood of the eternal covenant' (13:20; cf. 10:29). So the living and reigning Lord Jesus continues to be 'the mediator of a new covenant', and his 'sprinkled blood' continues to 'speak' from heaven of acceptance and forgiveness (12:22–24). Put another way, 'he is able to save to the uttermost those who draw near to God through him, since he always lives to make intercession for them' (7:25).

In 9:18–20 the writer compares the role of Moses and his use of blood to inaugurate 'the first covenant' (cf. Exod. 24:6–8). Hebrews goes on to discuss the importance of blood more extensively in the rites of that covenant and to contrast the singular and eternally effective sacrifice of Christ (9:21–28). As mediator and guarantor of the New Covenant, Jesus the messianic high priest realizes its benefits and secures its continuance and ultimate success.[8] This line of argument gives believers absolute assurance of God's continuing grace towards them.

---

6. Cf. O'Brien, *Hebrews*, p. 292; D. Sänger, *EDNT* 2:410–411.

7. Although the Old Testament mentions covenants made by God with Noah (Gen. 6:18; 9:9–17), Abraham (15:18; 17:2–14) and others, Hebrews restricts the term *diathēkē* to the covenant made with Israel at Sinai through the mediation of Moses (Exod. 19:5–6; 24:3–8) and the New Covenant. The author prefers to speak of God's *promises* to Abraham (6:13–15; 7:4–6; 11:8–12, 17–18) as the foundation of his relationship with Israel.

8. Lehne, *New Covenant*, p. 153, n. 76, rightly links both 'mediator' and 'guarantor' to the whole work of Jesus, not just to his sacrificial death.

The need

Better promises

Hebrews maintains that the covenant mediated by Christ is superior to the old one because it is 'enacted on better promises' (8:6). The word 'enacted' (*nenomothetētai*; cf. 7:11) implies that the New Covenant is a legal agreement, graciously imposed by God. Although it is based on promises, it demands a response. The first covenant was also based on promises, but the second is founded on 'better promises', providing a 'better hope . . . through which we draw near to God' (7:19).

God's promises to Abraham included the pledge to bless him and multiply his descendants (6:14; 11:12), and to give him an inheritance (11:8–10; cf. Gen. 12:1–3, 7). The Sinai Covenant was established on the basis of these same promises. God undertook to redeem the Israelites from slavery, to take them as his people and to bring them into the land he promised to their forefathers (Exod. 6:6–8). He would dwell among them and be their God (Exod. 29:25; Lev. 26:11–13). Israel's responsibility was to obey his voice and keep his covenant (Exod. 19:5).

Fundamental to the New Covenant is God's pledge 'to be their God, and they shall be my people'. God promises to renew the relationship at the heart of the Sinai Covenant. The surrounding promises indicate how this renewal will take place and how the relationship will be maintained. Hebrews 9:15 draws out the eschatological implications, claiming that a redemption has occurred that makes it possible for those who are called to receive 'the promised eternal inheritance'.

Israel's failure

When the writer cites Jeremiah's prophecy in full, he surrounds the quotation with statements about the imperfect and provisional nature of the first covenant. Initially, he claims that 'if that first covenant had been faultless, there would have been no occasion to look for a second' (8:7). Drawing attention to the blame contained within the oracle itself (8:8–9; Jer. 31:32), he asserts that God 'finds fault with them' when he reveals his intention to establish a new covenant. The accusation here explicitly concerns *the failure of God's people* ('for they did not continue in my covenant'). At the same time, God draws attention to *his judgment upon them* ('and so I showed no concern for them, declares the Lord').[9]

Implicitly, then, a major weakness of the Old Covenant was its inability to maintain the people in faithfulness to God and to prevent them from experiencing his wrath.[10] The writer has already asserted that 'perfection' was unattainable through the law and its provisions (7:11–19). Perhaps for this reason he uses the verb *synteleso* (complete) in 8:8, rather than *diathesomai* (establish), as in Jeremiah 38:31 LXX. God promises to complete or consummate a covenant that achieves the very best outcome for his people.[11]

The problem of sin

Elsewhere, Hebrews speaks about sin as the fundamental issue. Since the exodus generation hardened their heart in unbelief and disobedience, they could not continue in God's covenant and they experienced his judgment (3:7–19). Even though the priesthood and sacrificial system provided a way of cleansing and sanctification for later generations of Israelites (5:1–3; 7:27; 8:3), the effect was temporary and external (9:1–10; 10:1–4). There was no definitive forgiveness of sins, as promised under the New Covenant, and no way of

---

9. The Hebrew of Jer. 31:32 is stronger than the LXX in asserting their failure (ESV, 'my covenant that they broke'), but it affirms the Lord's continuing grace and faithfulness ('though I was their husband'), rather than his abandonment of them. The LXX reflects the theme of judgment found elsewhere in Jeremiah.

10. H. W. Attridge, *The Epistle to the Hebrews* (Philadelphia: Fortress, 1989), p. 227, unfairly criticizes Hebrews for disregarding the immediate context of Jeremiah's oracle, which is positive and hopeful. So also Lehne, *New Covenant*, p. 31. But this approach fails to perceive how Jer. 31:32 picks up the accusations of the prophet in earlier contexts and uses them to highlight the gracious intentions of God.

11. Cf. O'Brien, *Hebrews*, p. 297.

changing the heart of the people (10:15–18). Jesus came to make 'purification for sins' (1:3; 2:17; 7:27), 'to put away sin by the sacrifice of himself' (9:26, 28), and to sanctify and perfect a people for himself through the shedding of his blood in a single sacrifice for sins (10:10–14; 13:12).

So when the writer makes another negative assessment of the Old Covenant in 8:13, he observes that, when God speaks through the mouth of the prophet about a new covenant, 'he makes the first one obsolete'. In Jeremiah's oracle 'God himself declared that the Sinai covenant was unserviceable and outmoded.'[12] Certain that the New Covenant has been inaugurated by Christ, the writer concludes that 'what is becoming obsolete and growing old is ready to vanish away'. These themes are developed in the rest of Hebrews.

The promises fulfilled

Definitive forgiveness

There are two passages that particularly expand on the weaknesses and provisionality of the Old Covenant (9:1–10; 10:1–4). Each passage is followed by a section outlining the fulfilment and replacement of rituals and holy places in the work of Christ (9:11–14; 10:5–14). At the end of each sequence is a reference to the inauguration of the New Covenant and its effect (9:15–28; 10:15–18). In this way Hebrews 9 – 10 continues the emphases of Hebrews 7 – 8, pointing to the need for the New Covenant and showing how it brings perfection. True to the structure of Jeremiah's oracle, Hebrews shows how God being 'merciful towards their iniquities' and remembering their sins no more is foundational to the other benefits promised.

Forgiveness is mentioned only twice in Hebrews. In 9:22 it is claimed that 'under the law almost everything is purified with blood,

12. Ibid., p. 303. O'Brien, n. 86, observes that 'the idea that the Sinai covenant was temporary ran counter to Jewish sources, which regarded it as everlasting'.

and without the shedding of blood there is no forgiveness of sins'. In 10:18, when part of Jeremiah 31:34 has been cited for a second time, the writer declares that 'where there is forgiveness of these, there is no longer any offering for sin'. Both references support the argument that the promise of the New Covenant is fulfilled in the unique sacrifice of Jesus, which makes possible a complete cleansing or purification from sin and its consequences.

The writer follows his first citation from Jeremiah with a paragraph focusing on the regulations for worship and structure of the earthly sanctuary prescribed by God in the law given to Moses (9:1–10; cf. 8:5). He claims special insight from the Holy Spirit as he reflects on these provisions in the light of their fulfilment in Christ. As long as this whole system was in operation there was no real access to the presence of God (9:8; cf. 8:5; 9:24). Moreover, gifts and sacrifices that were offered were not able 'to perfect the worshipper with respect to conscience' (9:9, my tr.).[13] Such rituals dealt only with 'food and drink and various washings, regulations for the body imposed until the time of reformation' (9:10; cf. 10:3–4).

Hebrews uses the verb 'to perfect' (*teleiōsai*) in a vocational sense here, with reference to those who would worship or serve God (*latreuein*, as in 9:14; 10:2; 12:28).[14] An interesting parallel occurs in 10:1–2, where the writer points out that the sacrifices of the Old Covenant cannot 'make perfect those who draw near' (*tous proserchomenous teleiōsai*), and then observes, 'Otherwise, would they not have ceased to be offered, since the worshippers (*tous latreuontas*) having once been cleansed, would no longer have any consciousness

---

13. Although the Greek can be translated 'to perfect the conscience of the worshipper' (NIV, ESV), it is important to understand that the verb *teleiōsai* has 'the worshipper' as its direct object and that *kata syneidēsin* (with respect to conscience) signifies a particular sphere in which this perfecting must take place.

14. Cf. D. G. Peterson, *Hebrews and Perfection: An Examination of the Concept of Perfection in the 'Epistle to the Hebrews'*, SNTSMS 47 (Cambridge: Cambridge University Press, 1982), pp. 126–136.

of sins (*syneidēsin hamartiōn*)'.[15] It is the cleansing of the conscience that makes possible the perfecting of the worshipper, according to the next section of the argument (9:11–14).

With the appearance of Christ as 'a high priest of the good things that have come', what was foreshadowed in the Old Testament has become a reality (9:11; 10:1). Jesus has particularly fulfilled the role of the high priest on the annual Day of Atonement (9:7, 11–12; Lev. 16:1–19). When he ascended 'through the heavens' (4:14), he passed through 'the greater and more perfect tent (not made with hands, that is, not of this creation)', opening the way into the true sanctuary or 'heaven itself' (9:11, 24; cf. 8:1–2). So direct access to God, without any rituals or human intermediaries is now uniquely possible through Jesus and his sacrifice.

Jesus did not enter the heavenly presence of God by means of 'the blood of goats and calves but by means of his own blood' (9:12). Since his sacrifice was so perfect he entered the Most Holy Place 'once for all', thus 'securing an eternal redemption'. A similar expression in 9:15 indicates that this liberation is from the judgment and guilt produced by sin. 'Eternal redemption' is another way of speaking about the once-for-all and standing offer of forgiveness promised in Jeremiah 31:34.

The New Covenant inaugurated

It is often argued that in 9:16–17 the writer turns from using *diathēkē* in the Hebraic sense of 'covenant' to the Hellenistic sense of 'a last will and testament'. However, it is possible that the term is used consistently throughout 9:15–22, as the writer explains the need for a death to occur because of 'transgressions committed under the first covenant'. The covenant makers

---

15. The noun *syneidēsis* is normally translated 'conscience' (cf. 9:9, 14; 10:22; 13:18) and refers to that moral self-awareness of having done wrong. In 10:2 it is more simply used in a cognitive sense, with the whole expression conveying the notion of a guilty conscience (TNIV 'felt guilty for their sins'). Cf. C. Maurer, *TDNT* 7:898–907, p. 918.

had ritually invoked upon themselves the covenant curse of death.
Therefore, under these circumstances (where the covenant in
question had been ratified by a bloody oath ritual; cf. 9:18–22)
'it is necessary for the death of the covenant maker to be borne'.
(Heb. 9:16, my tr.)[16]

Such a reading of the text leads logically into the next section, where
Jesus fulfils his high-priestly role by acting as the Suffering Servant
'to bear the sins of many' (9:28; cf. Isa. 53:12). So Jesus inaugurates
the New Covenant by experiencing the curse that was upon those
who broke the Sinai Covenant.

In 9:23 – 10:14 Hebrews emphasizes the efficacy of Christ's once-
for-all sacrifice. Since he has 'put away sin by the sacrifice of himself'
(9:26), the benefits of the New Covenant are perpetually available to those who draw near to God through him. The law was
unable to sanctify and perfect in this way because it was 'but a
shadow of the good things to come instead of the true form of
these realities' (10:1). All that remains is for Jesus to return to 'save
those who are eagerly waiting for him' (9:28), and to see his enemies
made 'a footstool for his feet' (10:13; cf. Ps. 110:1).

When the writer draws the central doctrinal section of his
argument to a close, he clarifies again how this promise has been
fulfilled (10:15–18). An abbreviated summary of Jeremiah's oracle
recalls God's commitment to 'remember their sins and their lawless
deeds no more'. The writer then adds, 'Where there is forgiveness
of these, there is no longer any offering for sin.' Logically, such a
definitive forgiveness requires a unique and permanently effective
sacrifice for sin. This has been achieved by 'the offering of the body
of Jesus Christ once for all' (10:10, 12).

---

16. P. R. Williamson, *Sealed with an Oath: Covenant in God's Unfolding Purpose*,
    NSBT 23 (Downers Grove: InterVarsity Press; Nottingham: Apollos, 2007),
    p. 205, following S. W. Hahn, 'A Broken Covenant and the Curse of Death:
    A Study of Hebrews 9:15–22', *CBQ* 66 (2004), pp. 416–436. Williamson's
    translation of *pheresthai* (9:16) as 'to be borne' is much more natural than
    ESV, 'to be established'.

But what about the promise to transform hearts and renew the obedience of God's people (8:10; 10:16)? In what way does Hebrews envisage that God has acted to put his laws 'into their minds' and to 'write them on their hearts'?

Consciences cleansed for service to God

Mostly, the writer uses 'law' in connection with the requirements for priesthood, sacrifice and tabernacle under the Sinai Covenant (7:5, 12, 16, 19, 28; 8:4; 9:22; 10:1, 8), though every command of the law is included in 9:19 (cf. 10:28). When Jeremiah uses the plural 'laws' (Jer. 31:33), it is likely that God's moral and social commandments, as well as his provisions for cultic worship, are in view. Hebrews brings together the cultic, the moral and the social demands of the law in a new way, viewing the worship acceptable to God under the New Covenant as a whole-of-life response to his gracious initiative in Christ (9:14; 12:28 – 13:16).

Outlining the practical consequences of Christ's death, 9:13 asserts that ritual cleansing under the Old Covenant was for the benefit of those who were ceremonially unclean, to sanctify them by making them outwardly pure (*pros tēn tēs sarkos katharotēta*, 'for the purification of the flesh'). Those who were defiled could be restored to fellowship with God in the sense only that they were able to participate again in the Israelite cult.

The fundamental truth that blood 'purifies' and 'sanctifies', even if only at an external level, provides the basis for the 'how much more' argument in 9:14. 'The blood of Christ' is uniquely effective because he 'offered himself without blemish to God', alluding to Jesus' life of perfect obedience to the Father, culminating in the cross (cf. 5:7–9; 7:26–27; 10:10).[17] His sacrifice is able to 'purify our conscience from dead works', meaning from sins that defile the

---

17. 'Through the eternal Spirit' most likely refers to the power of the Holy Spirit upholding and maintaining him (cf. Isa. 42:1), though some would take it to mean his own spirit, highlighting the interior or spiritual quality of his sacrifice.

conscience and bring judgment,[18] so that we might 'serve the living
God'. A true and lasting consecration to God and his service is
thus implied.

The New Covenant promise of a renewed 'heart', based on a
decisive forgiveness of sins (Jer. 31:33–34), is echoed here. Although
Hebrews employs the word 'conscience' to describe the sphere of
inner transformation (*syneidēsis* in 9:9, 14; 10:2, 22; 13:18), it is closely
associated with the more Hebraic notion of the heart (*kardia*).[19]
Psalm 95:7–11 is cited to warn the readers not to harden their hearts
against God, as the Israelites did in the wilderness when they were
unbelieving and disobedient (3:7–19; 4:7). The word of God is able
to discern 'the thoughts and intentions of the heart', exposing
everyone 'to the eyes of him to whom we must give account' (4:12–
13). But those who have confidence in the finished work of Christ
can draw near to God 'with a true heart in full assurance of faith',
with their hearts 'sprinkled clean from an evil conscience' and their
bodies 'washed with pure water' (10:22).

A 'true heart' (*alēthinēs kardias*) demonstrates complete trust and
devotion towards God, as the following phrase indicates ('in full
assurance of faith'). Such a heart is completely different from 'an
evil, unbelieving heart, leading you to fall away from the living God'
(3:12). What makes such sincerity and loyalty possible is having
hearts 'sprinkled clean from an evil conscience'. The inauguration
of the Old Covenant was associated with the physical sprinkling of
the Israelites with blood (9:18–20; Exod. 24:6–8). Jesus' blood was
shed to inaugurate the New Covenant and is applied to the heart,
to cleanse consciences from guilt, when people believe the gospel

18. It is clear from 6:1 that 'repentance from dead works' means turning away
    from 'the practices and attitudes that belong to the way of death' (O'Brien,
    Hebrews, p. 325). But there also needs to be a cleansing of consciences from
    the guilt of such 'dead works' if a new covenant relationship with God is to
    be experienced.

19. C. Maurer, *TDNT* 7:908–919, rightly argues that OT teaching about the
    heart must be taken into account when evaluating what the NT means by
    conscience.

and trust that his sacrifice has made a full atonement for their sins (2:17; 9:26, 28). Having bodies washed with pure water is probably a reference to baptism as the outward sign of the 'sprinkling' of hearts.[20]

Only the cleansing provided by Jesus Christ can set believers free from condemnation and guilt to serve God with a new heart, as Jeremiah predicted. A later challenge to 'offer to God acceptable worship' (12:28–29), followed by a sequence of exhortations to live holy, loving and obedient lives (13:1–16), shows how the worship of the New Covenant is meant to be expressed in every sphere of life.[21] A transformation of human behaviour flows from a cleansing of the conscience and a renewing of the heart by God.

The writer talks specifically about the heart being 'strengthened by grace', rather than by foods and cultic rituals (13:9), and claims to have a 'good conscience' (*kalēn syneidēsin*), defining this in terms of 'desiring to act honourably in all things' (13:18, *en pasin kalōs thelontes anastrephesthai*).[22] So the heart is strengthened in God's ways by the gospel of grace, the conscience is set free from the burden of failure, and a new desire to please God is developed. In 6:4–5 Hebrews speaks about sharing in the Holy Spirit, but nowhere mentions the Spirit's role in transforming hearts. In view of other New Testament texts, we may conclude that the Spirit applies the gospel to the heart and conscience of the believer in such a way as

20. O'Brien, *Hebrews*, pp. 367–368, acknowledges that this is a possible understanding of 10:22, but prefers to view the sprinkling of the heart and the washing of the body as expressing the same thought, following the pattern of Ezek. 36:25–26.

21. Cf. D. G. Peterson, *Engaging with God: A Biblical Theology of Worship* (Leicester: Apollos; Downers Grove: InterVarsity Press, 1992), pp. 241–246.

22. O'Brien, *Hebrews*, p. 531, explains this as the firm resolve of the author and others 'to conduct themselves honourably as those summoned to holiness of life (12:14)'. Paul also speaks about having a 'good conscience', testifying to his godly manner of life (2 Cor. 1:12; Rom. 9:1), and writes to Timothy about believers having a good or pure conscience (1 Tim. 1:5, 19; 3:9; 2 Tim. 1:3).

to effect renewal and change (cf. 1 Cor. 2:10–13; 2 Cor. 3:16–18; 2 Thess. 2:13–14).

Drawing near to God through Jesus

Hebrews consistently represents worship as appropriate service to God, using the verb *latreuein* (8:5; 9:9, 14; 10:2; 12:28; 13:10) and the noun *latreia* (9:1, 6). The Sinai Covenant prescribed a pattern of service focused on an earthly sanctuary and dependent on the ministry of divinely appointed priests. This enabled God's people to 'draw near' to him in a formal and cultic sense, as they regularly engaged in rites of atonement, cleansing and consecration (10:1–2). Thus assured of God's presence with them and his covenant commitment to them (Exod. 29:42–46), they were encouraged to obey his commands in every sphere of life (Exod. 34:10–28).

However, 'the law made nothing perfect' (7:19). It was limited by a human priesthood, serving at a sanctuary that was only 'a copy and shadow' of 'the true tent that the Lord set up' (8:1–5), involving the repetition of sacrifices that could not definitively cleanse and sanctify the people or actually take away sins (10:1–4). Moreover, as the prophets discerned, this whole system of worship could not change the heart of the people and set them free from sin to serve God as they should. Hebrews adds that this method of relating to God could not bring those who were called to share in 'the promised eternal inheritance' (9:15; 11:39–40).

With the high-priestly ministry of Jesus, 'a better hope is introduced, though which we draw near to God' (7:19). Believers can approach God through Jesus with confidence to 'receive mercy and find grace to help in time of need' (4:14–16). They can be saved 'to the uttermost' by drawing near to God through him (7:25). They can be 'perfected for all time' because of his single sacrifice for sin and his heavenly exaltation (10:12–14; 12:22–24). The 'better hope' that the New Covenant provides ultimately involves sharing his glory (2:10), entering God's rest (4:11), seeing the Lord (12:14) and inhabiting the heavenly city (13:14). Meanwhile, the promises of God and the work of Christ provide hope of being sustained in that relationship until final glorification. 'The certainty of the actualisation of the drawing near is now stronger and surer and more complete than in the OT and later Judaism.'[23]

Knowing the Lord

Jeremiah predicted that they shall no longer 'teach his neighbour and each his brother, saying, "Know the LORD," for they shall all know me, from the least of them to the greatest' (Jer. 31:34). This knowledge is specifically related to God's promise that he would 'forgive their iniquity' and 'remember their sin no more'. Such knowledge of God is a key to the transformation of heart and mind that Jeremiah believed would issue in covenant loyalty and obedience to God's will.

Hebrews picks up the theme of knowing the Lord from the opening paragraph. God who 'spoke to our fathers by the prophets', in these last days 'has spoken to us by his Son' (1:1–2). Verbal revelation is included in the writer's perspective (2:3), but he draws immediate attention to the manifestation of God's glory, nature and power in the person and work of the Lord Jesus (1:3–4). At the heart of this revelation is his ministry of 'making purification for sins' and his subsequent exaltation to 'the right hand of the Majesty on high'. Here the writer announces the great gospel events that will be expounded as a manifestation of God's grace and the means by which he fulfils his eschatological plan and brings many 'sons' to glory (2:10).

There is an early insistence on the need to 'pay much closer attention to what we have heard, lest we drift away from it' (2:1), introducing the note of warning that surfaces at several key points in the argument. This is followed by a challenge to those who 'share in a heavenly calling' to 'consider Jesus, the apostle and high priest of our confession' (3:1). The message originally received by

---

23. H. Preisker, *TDNT* 2:331. Note that the word *parrēsia* (confidence) is used to describe the approach that Christians can have to God (4:16; 10:19) and the hope they have (3:6). Such confidence should not be thrown away or easily abandoned (10:35)! Cf. Peterson, *Perfection*, pp. 79–80.

the readers was focused on Jesus as *revealer* of God's character and will and as *high priest* of the New Covenant.[24] So the writer's 'word of exhortation' (13:22) is a development and application of the message that brought them to Jesus in the first place. They need to consider his faithfulness to God and their status as 'his house', if they are to hold fast their confidence and hope (3:2–6).

This warning is developed as the writer addresses the problem of apostasy in more detail (3:7 – 4:10). Psalm 95:7–11 is cited, with its reflection on the unbelief and disobedience of the wilderness generation, who always went astray 'in their heart' because they did not know God's ways. The readers are urged to take care

> lest there be in any of you an evil, unbelieving heart, leading you to fall away from the living God. But exhort one another every day as long as it is called 'today', that none of you may be hardened by the deceitfulness of sin. (3:12–13)

Their mutual exhortation was doubtless meant to follow the pattern of the writer's own exhortation to them, recalling and explaining the significance of God's saving work through his Son, and challenging them to faithfulness and perseverance on the basis of their God-given hope.

In terms of Jeremiah's promise, Hebrews implies that the readers have a knowledge of the Lord and his grace that should sustain them in their relationship with him and bring them to their heavenly destination. But he is concerned that they should have a deeper understanding of gospel truths, be stirred to avoid sin, stand firm in times of testing, and be encouraged to realize in everyday experience the benefits won for them by Jesus (4:14–16).

---

24. This 'confession' (*homologia*) appears to be a core statement of what the readers believed and therefore confessed. In 4:14–16, where this is mentioned again, Jesus is identified as high priest and Son of God (cf. 10:19–23). 'Apostle' in 3:1 probably refers to Jesus as the one sent from God to reveal him and so corresponds to 'Son of God' in 4:14. Cf. O'Brien, *Hebrews*, pp. 129–131.

Put another way, he wants them to mature in their relationship with God. They have become 'dull of hearing' (5:11, *nōthroi tais akoais*) and he fears that they may be unwilling to receive the sort of teaching he wants to give them and respond appropriately.[25] A particular sign of their spiritual sluggishness is their unwillingness to be 'teachers'. After a certain time, anyone instructed in the faith ought to be able to explain and apply it to others, even in a simple and basic way (5:12; cf. 3:13; 10:24–25). 'They stand in need of renewed commitment and obedience to Christ, based upon deeper insight into what they profess.'[26]

The writer assesses that they need to be taught all over again 'the basic principles of the oracles of God' (5:12, *ta stoicheia tēs archēs tōn logiōn tou theou*). This could mean that they still needed guidance about how to interpret the Old Testament from a Christian perspective. More specifically, the expression may be a parallel to what 6:1 describes as 'the elementary doctrine of Christ' (*ton tēs archēs tou Christou logon*). Such fundamental teaching is identified as 'milk, not solid food'.

As in the physical realm, spiritual 'milk' is for infants and 'solid food is for the mature' (5:14). Despite their immaturity, the writer goes on to give them solid food. By implication, people can be brought to maturity only by giving them a taste for the food that sustains and strengthens the mature. The problem with spiritual infancy is being 'unskilled in the word of righteousness' (5:13, *apeiros logou dikaiosynēs*). When mature Christians are described in 5:14, they are said to have 'their powers of discernment trained by constant practice to distinguish good from evil' (5:14). This suggests spiritual discernment with a moral outcome. Both expressions highlight the need to 'follow through on the implications of their Christian confession, and be ready to be trained by God's discipline because

---

25. In 6:12 the writer uses the word *nōthroi* again, but in an unqualified way, suggesting that a persistent unwillingness to receive solid teaching and act upon it may lead to complete sluggishness or apostasy (as defined in 6:4–6).

26. O'Brien, *Hebrews*, p. 206.

of the harvest of righteousness and peace that are produced by it
(12:10–11)'.[27]

When the writer urges them to 'leave the elementary doctrine of
Christ and go on to maturity' (6:1), he does not mean abandon
fundamental teaching altogether. His challenge is qualified by what
follows: 'not laying again a foundation of repentance from dead
works and of faith toward God, and of instruction about washings,
the laying on of hands, the resurrection of the dead, and eternal
judgment'. They need to build upon the foundations already laid
and work out the implications of the teaching already given. The
solid food the writer gives them involves a development of the
themes of repentance and faith, resurrection from the dead and
eternal judgment, explained in the light of the high-priestly ministry
of Jesus.[28]

In short, then, they do not need to say to one another, 'Know
the Lord,' since their common experience is the result of coming
to know God in a new way through the person and work of his Son.
They do know him, 'from the least of them to the greatest'! But they
need to press on in that knowledge, working out the implications
of their relationship with God together, holding fast to the hope
they have been given, even in the face of persecution and severe
testing, and stirring up one another to love and good works (10:19–
25, 32–39). In this context, they need to teach and exhort one
another, and all the more as they see the Day of Christ's return
approaching (10:25).

---

27. Ibid., p. 210. Cf. Peterson, *Perfection*, pp. 181–182.
28. Even 'washings' come up for further consideration in 9:10, 13–14; 10:22.
    W. Manson, *The Epistle to the Hebrews* (London: Hodder & Stoughton,
    1951), pp. 15–16, suggests that 'the danger to their faith lay not in their
    return to Judaism as such, but in a retardation of their Christian progress
    by factors having their causes in the Jewish element in their Christianity,
    in other words, by an undue assertion of their Jewish-Christian
    inheritance'.

Eschatology and the New Covenant

The New Covenant needs to be understood in the light of the writer's inaugurated eschatology. 'In these last days' Jesus made purification for sin and was exalted to the Father's right hand (1:2–3; cf. 9:26, 'at the end of the ages'). Cleansing and forgiveness have become perpetually available and a new knowledge of God has been made possible, transforming hearts and minds and enabling God's people to serve him acceptably. But the full realization of these benefits awaits the return of Jesus and 'the world to come' (2:5; cf. 4:9; 9:28; 13:14), where there will be

> unfettered mutual fellowship between God and men, the creation of a community in which not only is there no need for instruction but no breach of fellowship occurs, no divisions within the new community are expected.[29]

Exhortations and warnings

In this waiting time those who are beneficiaries of the New Covenant need to be warned about the danger of drifting from the message that brought them to faith (2:1–4), hardening their hearts in unbelief and disobedience and turning away from the living God (3:7 – 4:11). Positively, they need to hold fast to the confidence and hope given to them in the gospel (3:6), looking to their faithful Lord (3:1–5; 10:23; 12:1–2), and exhorting one another not to be hardened by the deceitfulness of sin (3:12–14). They need to become 'imitators of those who through faith and patience inherit the promises' (6:12; 11:4–38), encouraging one another to pursue love and good works (10:24–25). Negatively, they need to be warned by the example of

---

29. W. J. Dumbrell, *Covenant and Creation: A Theology of the Old Testament Covenants* (Exeter: Paternoster, 1984), pp. 181–183. Cf. Williamson, *Sealed with an Oath*, pp. 208–210. Dumbrell argues that Jeremiah looks 'beyond the New Testament age to the community of the end-time, to a situation when the kingdom of God has finally come and God is all in all'.

those who failed to persevere in faith, hope and love (3:7 – 4:11; 12:15–17).

There is an intensification of warning in 6:4–6, as the writer comes to describe what it means to 'fall away' (6:6, *parapesontas*; cf. 3:12, *apostēnai*). Ultimately, such people make a deliberate stand against Christ, 'crucifying once again the Son of God to their own harm and holding him up to contempt'. Treating him as his executioners did, they openly put themselves in the position of his enemies. They deny the need for his sacrifice and oppose those who proclaim it. But can genuine Christians become apostate?

The context certainly suggests that those who fall away have the appearance of being converted. They have 'once been enlightened', suggesting that the light of the gospel has shone into their lives (6:4; cf. 10:32). They have 'tasted the heavenly gift', which may mean receiving Christ himself and all the spiritual blessings he offers.[30] They have 'shared in the Holy Spirit' (literally, 'having become partakers of the Holy Spirit', *metochous genēthentas pneumatos hagiou*) and have 'tasted the goodness of the word of God and the powers of the age to come' (6:5; cf. 2:4). This suggests a decisive experience of the benefits of the New Covenant.

However, those who have enjoyed such a relationship with God cannot presume on that relationship, believing themselves to be immune from the possibility of apostasy. If they are genuine partakers of Christ and his Spirit, they will demonstrate that by maintaining their faith in him and all that he has accomplished 'to the end' (3:6, 14). In dogmatic terms, God will enable the elect to persevere in faith and good works. Consequently, those who are truly the brothers and sisters of Christ (2:11–12) and the 'children' whom God has given him (2:13) will identify themselves

---

30. 'Tasting' implies experiencing something in a manner that is real and personal (not merely 'sipping'), as in 2:9 ('that he might taste death for everyone'). Attridge, *Hebrews*, p. 170, for example, argues that 6:4–5 describes 'the initial experience of conversion and life in the eschatological community'.

by continuing to express the Christ-focused confidence he has given them.[31]

The writer believes that a true work of God has taken place in the congregation he addresses (6:9; 10:39), 'but this does not exclude the possibility that some of their number are rebellious at heart and, unless there is a radical change, will find that they have reached the point of irremediable apostasy'.[32] People can be caught up in a group experience, without being genuinely converted. As Jesus taught in the parable of the soils, some responses to the gospel can be superficial and temporary, even though they appear to be genuine at first (cf. Mark 4:14–19).[33] Hebrews has in view those who see clearly where the truth lies, conform to it for a while, and then, for various reasons, renounce it.

The fearful consequence of apostasy

A warning passage in 10:26–31 returns to the theme of apostasy, describing it as 'sinning deliberately after receiving the knowledge of the truth' (cf. 6:4).[34] For such people, 'there no longer remains a sacrifice for sins, but a fearful expectation of judgment, and a fury of fire that will consume the adversaries'. Recalling the argument

---

31. Cf. T. R. Schreiner and A. B. Caneday, *The Race Set Before Us: A Biblical Theology of Perseverance and Assurance* (Downers Grove: InterVarsity Press; Leicester: IVP, 2001). H. W. Bateman IV (ed.), *Four Views on the Warning Passages in Hebrews* (Grand Rapids: Kregel, 2007), provides a discussion between Reformed and Arminian theologians on this issue.

32. P. E. Hughes, *A Commentary on the Epistle to the Hebrews* (Grand Rapids: Eerdmans, 1977), p. 212. Hughes notes that Hebrews consistently uses some variation of the expression 'any of you' (3:12–13; 4:1) or simply the word 'any' or 'some' (*tis*; cf. 4:11; 10:25; 12:15–16) in addressing the group as a whole.

33. Cf. C. A. Thomas, *A Case for Mixed-Audience with Reference to the Warning Passages in the Book of Hebrews* (New York: Peter Lang, 2008).

34. 'Sinning deliberately' recalls the distinction made in Num. 15 between those who unintentionally disobeyed God's commands (vv. 22–29) and those who sinned defiantly ('with a high hand') and had to be cut off from the people because they 'despised the word of the Lord' (vv. 30–31).

about Jesus' once-for-all sacrifice for sins, the writer insists that there is no hope of salvation for those who reject him and the covenant he has inaugurated. Those who do so will share the fate of those who never accepted him in the first place. If Israelites who rejected the law of Moses died without mercy on the evidence of two or three witnesses (Deut. 17:2–7), how much more will those who persist in rejecting the Son of God experience his judgment (cf. 2:1–4)!

Anyone who has 'spurned the Son of God' has 'profaned the blood of the covenant by which he was sanctified' (10:29). 'The blood of the covenant' was mentioned in 9:20, where Exodus 24:8 is cited. Now the writer applies the term to the New Covenant, affirming that Jesus' blood brings believers into the sanctified relationship with God that Jeremiah envisaged, consecrating them to his service (10:10; 13:12).

The New Covenant is later called 'the eternal covenant' (13:20), because it is based on 'an eternal redemption' (9:12), making it possible for believers to receive 'the promised eternal inheritance' (9:15). But its operation is not mechanical, providing salvation to those who spurn the grace of God. To abandon trust in the Son of God and his sacrifice for sin is to treat his blood as common or unclean (10:29, *koinon*). To do so is also to insult 'the Spirit of grace', who was active in the ministry of Jesus (9:14), and who confirms the truth of the gospel (2:3–4), enabling people to experience its benefits (6:4–5).

It is God's role to avenge or repay sin of every kind (Deut. 32:35) and God has specifically revealed that he will judge his people (Deut. 32:36), vindicating the true by removing the false. The writer concludes from this that 'it is a fearful thing to fall into the hands of the living God' (Heb. 10:31). Such language has affinities with the covenantal curses of Deuteronomy 28 – 29, suggesting that there are even more serious consequences for rejecting Jesus and the New Covenant.

Once again, serious warning is followed by an expression of confidence in those addressed and an encouragement to persevere

(10:35–39). Based on the writer's perception of the faith, hope and love they demonstrated in the past, he urges them not to abandon their trust in what God has promised and shrink back from faith in him so as to be 'lost'.

Responding to the call of God

When Israel gathered at Mount Sinai, to hear the voice of God, it was a terrifying occasion (12:18–21; cf. Exod. 19), moving the people to beg that no further word be spoken to them. Christians, on the other hand, have come to 'Mount Zion and to the city of the living God, the heavenly Jerusalem' (cf. Gal. 4:26; Rev. 21:2). In their conversion, they have come to God, 'the judge of all', and to a joyful assembly of angels with the perfected saints of all generations (12:22–24).[35] The emphasis here is on *acceptance* because of 'Jesus, the mediator of a new covenant', and his 'sprinkled blood that speaks a better word than the blood of Abel' (cf. 11:4). Jesus has opened the way into the heavenly sanctuary for his followers (6:19–20; 10:19–20), 'and they enjoy proleptic access to the heavenly realities; yet the old age has not completely given way to the new'.[36] They still seek 'the city that is to come' (13:14).

The notion of God speaking continues in the next section (12:25–27). There is no reason to 'refuse him who is speaking' or to 'reject him who warns from heaven'. God continues to speak through the gospel about his gracious provision for sin, making membership of his eschatological people possible. Nevertheless, if the Israelites did not escape God's condemnation when they turned away from him, 'much less will we' (cf. 2:1–4). When God spoke from Sinai, the whole mountain trembled violently (Exod. 19:18). The curse

---

35. Cf. Peterson, *Perfection*, pp. 160–166. This passage summarizes in a visionary way many of the themes presented earlier in Hebrews. O'Brien, *Hebrews*, p. 478, notes how the transition from 12:18–24 to the warning passage of 12:25–29 continues the writer's pattern of moving rhetorically from exposition to exhortation.

36. Lehne, *New Covenant*, p. 100. However, 12:22–24 stresses *membership* of the heavenly company, not simply access to God.

sanctions of the covenant were effective and that first generation perished in the wilderness (cf. 3:16–19). Haggai 2:6 promises that when it is time for the final judgment and the end of this world-order, God will shake 'not only the earth but also the heavens' (12:26). All that will remain is what cannot be shaken (12:27), namely the kingdom that Christ shares with those who continue to trust in him (12:28).

Certainty about God's provision of an unshakable kingdom should motivate believers to a life of gratitude and acceptable worship (12:28–29). As already noted, this means serving God with faithfulness and obedience in every aspect of life (13:1–16). However, acceptable worship is characterized by 'reverence and awe', since 'our God is a consuming fire'. This alludes to Deuteronomy 4:24 (cf. Deut. 9:3; Isa. 33:14), where the Israelites were warned not to indulge in idolatry, but to remain faithful to the Lord and to serve him exclusively, lest they provoke him to anger. The certainty of God's grace must never blind us to the truth that a terrible judgment awaits the apostate (cf. 2:2–3; 6:4–8; 12:14–17).

Conclusion

The writer's portrayal of Jesus as high priest of a new covenant order is 'a deliberate reformulation of the Christian story in response to specific needs of his audience'.[37] They seem to have had a longing to incorporate into their lives some form of Jewish cultic observance (cf. 7:11; 9:8–10, 13–14; 10:1–10; 13:9–14). Although commentators generally agree that they were Jewish-Christian believers, there is disagreement about their exact circumstances and the nature of their struggle.[38] They are urged to see themselves as the renewed people of God, the recipients of the New Covenant promised to 'the house

---

37. Lehne, *New Covenant*, p. 17. She rightly observes that for the people of the New Covenant 'the "imperative" of cultic service in the new order is grounded in the (prior) "indicative" of their salvation in Christ'.

38. Cf. Attridge, *Hebrews*, pp. 9–13; O'Brien, *Hebrews*, pp. 9–13.

of Israel' and 'the house of Judah'.[39] Gentile believers are not
mentioned, though their inclusion in the blessings could be implied
by the expression 'offspring of Abraham' (2:16).

Although the recipients of Hebrews admirably endured suffering
and persecution soon after turning to Christ (10:32–34), they needed
to be strengthened to stand firm in any future trial (10:35–39;
12:1–13). Part of the problem seems to have been the unwillingness
of some to mature in their understanding and move on in their
obedience to God (5:11 – 6:12; 12:28 – 13:17). Failing to grasp the
implications of Jesus' coming for the fulfilment of Scripture and
the furtherance of God's saving plan, they wanted to retreat into a
compromised form of Christianity to avoid harassment and struggle.
But from the writer's point of view this was potentially a pathway
to apostasy.

Contemporary readers may find the argument about the Mosaic
law and its fulfilment in Christ difficult to follow and foreign to their
life situation. We are mostly Gentile believers, who have been caught
up in the story of Israel many generations after the messianic transformation of the people of God was initiated. The writer's
exhortations are much easier to understand and apply. There is no
escaping the relevance of the warning passages and the positive
encouragements that accompany them. But theological exposition
is in the service of exhortation in Hebrews, and especially so as
the writer explains how the promises of the New Covenant have
been fulfilled.

We need to understand how the death and heavenly exaltation
of Jesus achieve a solution to the problem of sin, requiring no
religious activity or any other form of mediation to secure the
salvation of God's people. The knowledge of God and his grace

---

39. R. B. Hays, '"Here We Have No Lasting City": New Covenantalism in
    Hebrews', in R. Bauckham, D. R. Driver, T. A. Hart and N. MacDonald
    (eds.), *The Epistle to the Hebrews and Christian Theology* (Grand Rapids:
    Eerdmans, 2009), pp. 151–173, argues that Hebrews is no more
    supersessionist than Jeremiah: Hebrews is not about the rejection, but
    the restoration, of Israel.

that Jesus brings is truly life-transforming and sufficient to sustain believers in their relationship with God 'firm to the end' (3:14). This redemptive knowledge of God changes hearts and minds, setting them free from 'dead works to serve the living God' (9:14). Continually drawing near to God through Jesus as our heavenly high priest, to receive mercy and 'grace to help in time of need' (4:16), is critical for the maintenance of this relationship. Such an ongoing realization of the benefits of the New Covenant will facilitate perseverance in faith, hope and love (6:10–12; 10:23–25).

The antidote to immaturity, spiritual apathy and regression is to receive the 'solid food' the writer offers, allowing the knowledge of God it conveys to draw us on to realize the 'full assurance of hope until the end' (6:11). In practical terms, this means letting the Christian hope control thinking and behaviour in the present. Our hope is based on the promises of God, confirmed with an oath. God's plan for us has already been fulfilled in the death and heavenly exaltation of the Lord Jesus Christ, but there is a time of waiting in hope and persevering in grateful service before Jesus returns and brings us to the consummation of God's New Covenant plan.

Pastorally, Hebrews shows the importance of combining warning with assurance, urging believers to press on in the knowledge of God and his grace given to them in the gospel. In terms of Jeremiah's oracle, the assurance of sins forgiven through the finished work of Christ is primary. As believers grow in their understanding and appreciation of his high-priestly ministry, they need to appropriate the benefits on a daily basis.

New Covenant ministry requires an ongoing application of the gospel about Christ's redemptive work to the conscience of believers. With such an assurance of God's mercy, hearts are moved by gratitude and confidence to serve God and persevere in faithfulness. Such a ministry may take place in one-to-one situations or in small groups. It should certainly characterize the public gatherings of Christ's people, as they meet together to draw near to God, to express their confidence in his promises and to consider 'how to stir up one another to love and good works' (10:24).

Being in a New Covenant relationship with God means responding in faith hope and love to his gracious promises. Knowing God through Jesus Christ is not a static and purely intellectual experience. God's work in our hearts makes it possible for us to persevere in faith, hold unswervingly to the hope we profess, and keep on loving one another as he directs. But hearts that are strengthened and stimulated by his grace need to respond. Passive reliance on God and what he has accomplished for us through his Son falls short of the sort of relationship the New Covenant makes possible and God himself desires.

4. NEW COVENANT MINISTRY

There are two contexts in which the apostle Paul explicitly refers to the New Covenant.[1] In 1 Corinthians 11:25, he records the Last Supper saying of Jesus, 'This cup is the new covenant in my blood. Do this, as often as you drink it, in remembrance of me.'[2] This indicates that the sacrifice of Christ inaugurates the New Covenant by dealing definitively with the problem of human sin. As Paul says later in this letter, 'Christ died for our sins in accordance with the Scriptures' (1 Cor. 15:3). The foundational promise of Jeremiah's oracle is fulfilled in the Messiah's death for his people.

The New Covenant is mentioned again when Paul engages in an extensive defence of his ministry in 2 Corinthians 2:14 – 7:4. In this

---

1. Allusions to Jeremiah's prophecy of the New Covenant elsewhere in Paul's writings will be discussed in chapter 5.

2. This saying is close in form to Luke 22:20. But Luke's cup word includes no command to 'Do this, as often as you drink it, in remembrance of me,' and it includes the adjectival clause 'which is poured out for you'. Note my discussion of textual variations and different forms of this on pp. 57–58.

context the transformation of lives made possible by the New
Covenant is the focus, with echoes of Jeremiah's prophecy in the
expression 'written on our hearts' (3:2). The apostle goes on to speak
about God's reconciling work in the death of Christ as the basis of
his 'ministry of righteousness' (3:9) or 'ministry of reconciliation'
(5:18–21). This explains how Jeremiah's promise of a definitive
forgiveness of sins is experienced and passed on to others. However,
the benefits of the New Covenant are mostly expounded in
2 Corinthians 3 in terms of the work of the Holy Spirit. At this
point the predictions of Ezekiel 11:19–20 and 36:26–27 are used in
an intertextual way to explain how Jeremiah's promise of spiritual
renewal has been fulfilled.

A competency from God

Suffering for the gospel

Paul begins the defence of his ministry with a thanksgiving to God,
employing a metaphor that combines elements of *suffering* and
triumph. God is thanked for leading Paul in his victory procession,
so that through his preaching and life the apostle spreads the
fragrance of the knowledge of Christ everywhere he goes (2:14).
But the bearer of this 'fragrance' suffers in the course of his ministry
(cf. 1:8–10; 2:4; 2:12–13). Indeed, he sees himself sharing abundantly
in Christ's sufferings (1:5), making him specifically 'the aroma of
Christ to God among those who are being saved and among those
who are perishing' (2:15). Like the aroma of sacrificial victims under
the Mosaic Law (Lev. 1:9, 13, 17; 2:2), his sacrifice is pleasing to
God.[3] But at the human level his preaching divides people into one

---

3. P. Barnett, *The Second Epistle to the Corinthians*, NICNT (Grand Rapids:
    Eerdmans, 1997), p. 153, observes that 'it is Paul as the *proclaimer* of Christ
    crucified, and who as a consequence suffers, who is the aroma of Christ.
    The personally powerful fragrance-aroma imagery of vv. 14–16 is controlled
    by the immediate context, which began with his reference to coming to
    Troas "for the gospel of Christ".'

of two groups, 'those who are being saved' and 'those who are perishing' (cf. 1 Cor. 1:18).

Paul expands on this theme by saying that to those who are perishing he is 'a fragrance from death to death', but to those who are being saved he is 'a fragrance from life to life' (2 Cor. 2:16).

> The 'fragrance' of the death of Christ smelled in the apostolic herald by those who reject Christ crucified is 'unto death', a sign of their own eternal 'death'. The 'fragrance' of the risen Christ smelled in the apostle by those who turn to Christ is 'unto life', a sign of their own eternal 'life'.[4]

The implications of his calling are so awesome that the apostle asks, 'Who is sufficient for these things?' (2:16). He does not answer the question immediately, but contrasts himself with others whom he describes as literally 'peddling God's word'.[5] At the same time, he identifies himself with 'men of sincerity', who are commissioned by God and who in the sight of God 'speak in Christ' (2:17). As the argument develops, Paul finally claims that his sufficiency is from God, 'who has made us competent to be ministers of a new covenant' (3:5–6).

Opposing false gospels

Scholars have reconstructed the teaching and emphases of these 'peddlers of God's word' in different ways. Some have argued from later chapters that they presented themselves as 'divine men', who possessed superhuman traits including wisdom and the ability to work miracles. Others have proposed that they were Christian Jews from Jerusalem, who misrepresented the position of James and Peter and made much of visionary experiences and glossolalia. Care must be taken in using the 'mirror technique' of deriving

---

4. Ibid., p. 154.

5. The Greek (*kapēleuontes ton logon tou theou*) could indicate two things: they have diluted the message and have made money out of selling an inferior product. Cf. R. P. Martin, *2 Corinthians*, WBC 40 (Waco: Word, 1986), pp. 49–50.

information about Paul's rivals from an examination of what he espouses or critiques in the letter. For example, it cannot simply be assumed from 2 Corinthians 10 – 13 that they used Spirit-inspired visions and revelations to legitimate their ministry.[6] However, it is valid to ask why he argues as he does when dealing with alternative views.

The first context in which Paul engages with their position is 2 Corinthians 3 – 4. He begins the attack by reminding the Corinthians that his rivals needed 'letters of recommendation' to authorize their ministry:

> Are we beginning to commend ourselves again? Or do we need, as some do, letters of recommendation to you, or from you? You yourselves are our letter of recommendation, written on our hearts, to be known and read by all. And you show that you are a letter from Christ delivered by us, written not with ink but with the Spirit of the living God, not on tablets of stone but on tablets of human hearts. (3:1–3)

Echoing the language of Jeremiah 31:33 ('written on our hearts'), the apostle also draws on Ezekiel to identify 'the Spirit of the living God' as the agent of transformation. The hearts of Paul and his converts were affected as he brought them the blessings of the New Covenant.[7] He was drawn into an affectionate relationship with

---

6. Cf. T. R. Blanton, 'Spirit and Covenant Renewal: A Theologoumenon of Paul's Opponents in 2 Corinthians', *JBL* 129 (2010), pp. 129–134. Blanton, pp. 147–150, argues that Paul adduces manifestations of the Spirit as a means of legitimating his ministry, but not because his opponents made much of ecstatic or revelatory experiences. However, in view of the anti-triumphal tone he adopts in 2:14–17 and 11:1 – 12:21, it is hard to believe that he is not responding to rival claims about such experiences.

7. Although *hymōn* (your) is read by several manuscripts, the overall evidence favours reading *hēmōn* (our) in 3:2. The latter is consistent with Paul's claim in 7:3 ('you are in our hearts'). Cf. B. M. Metzger (ed.), *A Textual Commentary on the Greek New Testament*, 2nd ed. (Stuttgart: Deutsche Bibelgesellschaft, 1994), p. 509.

them, while they became a testimony to the divine power at work through his ministry.

The apologetic dimension to the argument in 3:1–3 is clear: 'Paul can point to a letter of introduction (the Corinthian church) written by a third party (Christ), who is a supernaturally higher authority, in which, however, he (Paul) has played a critical role.'[8] This gives an extraordinary significance to authentic gospel ministry. Polemically, the implication is that his rivals have only letters of recommendation written by human authorities with pen and ink, whereas he is directed and empowered by the Holy Spirit and the effect is seen in the lives of his converts.

Paul's polemic continues with the claim that the Spirit of God has written 'not on tablets of stone but on tablets of human hearts' (*en plaxin kardiais sarkinais*). Ezekiel 11:19 and 36:26 promise 'a heart of flesh' (*kardian sarkinēn*) instead of 'a heart of stone' (*tēn kardian tēn lithinēn*). Paul modifies the last term to read 'tablets of stone' (*plaxin lithinais*), preparing for the argument that the law given to Moses was 'carved in letters of stone' (3:7; cf. Exod. 31:18; 32:15; 34:1, 4).[9] Paul's ministry of the gospel has made it possible for the Spirit to write his directions on the softened hearts of those who belong to Christ.

Going on to describe what it means to be 'ministers of a new covenant', he insists that this covenant is 'not of the letter but of the Spirit. For the letter kills, but the Spirit gives life' (3:6; cf. Rom. 7:4–6). Although his opponents may have considered themselves to be 'ministers of a new covenant', as I argue below, they appear to have been teaching that this covenant involved a new ability to

---

8. Barnett, *Second Corinthians*, pp. 167–168. Their Spirit-filled assembly came about through Paul's preaching of the Son of God to them (1:18–22).

9. In 3:3 Paul is probably also anticipating the argument in 3:14–15 about minds and hearts being hardened against Moses and the Old Covenant. 'Disobedience to God's laws has desensitized "hearts of flesh" so as to become "tablets of stone"; the Law of God is as dead within them as their own dead hearts' (Barnett, *Second Corinthians*, p. 169).

keep the law of Moses.[10] Paul's point is that the letter 'kills' and
'condemns' (3:9) because it is a revelation that demands obedience
without the Spirit's empowerment. Only the Spirit can bring
hardened hearts to life and move people to please God.[11]

The glory of the New Covenant

Surpassing the Old Covenant
Paul's use of Exodus 34:29–35 in 2 Corinthians 3:7–18 suggests that
his opponents viewed the law of Moses as undiminished in glory
and still applicable to Christians. They are later described as 'super
apostles' (11:5; 12:11) or as 'false apostles' (11:13), who preach
'another Jesus' (11:4). Like Paul, they were Greek-speaking Jews
(11:22), possibly from Jerusalem, who claimed to be 'ministers of
Christ' (11:23) and 'minsters of righteousness' (11:15). But they came
to minister the righteousness associated with the law of Moses,
rather than the righteousness issuing in reconciliation with God
based on Christ's death (3:9; 5:21), which was the ministry of Paul.[12]

---

10. Cf. Blanton, 'Spirit and Covenant Renewal', pp. 144–147. Blanton, p. 148,
    proposes that when Paul dissociates the New Covenant from law here, he
    moves away from the position of Jeremiah, Ezekiel and later Jewish texts.
    However, as I have argued in chapter 1, Jeremiah was speaking about a
    more profound change of attitude and behavior than the phrase
    'internalisation of the law' suggests.

11. G. D. Fee, *God's Empowering Presence: The Holy Spirit in the Letters of Paul*
    (Peabody: Hendrickson, 1994), pp. 305–306, argues that Paul's contrast
    between letter and Spirit is eschatological, so that the coming of the Spirit
    brings fulfilment in the sense that 'what the law requires is now written on
    the heart' of God's people. Paul does not actually use the word 'law' (*nomos*)
    in this letter, but 'the letter', 'the old covenant' and 'Moses' are pointed
    substitutes (3:6–7, 14–15).

12. Cf. Barnett, *Second Corinthians*, pp. 34–40. Barnett, p. 179, n. 4, agrees that
    they could have used Exod. 34:29–35 against Paul, but argues that this
    opinion is 'inaccessible to analysis'. Cf. 1QS 1.5; Wisdom 2.11; *Psalms of
    Solomon* 8.6–10, and n. 15 below.

The apostle has already claimed that his New Covenant ministry is superior to Moses' ministry, which was associated with 'tablets of stone' (3:3) and 'the letter' of the law (3:6). Now he claims that the glory of the older dispensation has been surpassed by the glory of the newer one.

The word 'glory' appears ten times in Paul's comparison between the covenants.[13] Sometimes the antitheses are stark – 'the ministry of death, carved in letters of stone' is contrasted with the life-giving 'ministry of the Spirit' (3:7–8), 'the ministry of condemnation' with 'the ministry of righteousness' (3:9), 'what was being brought to an end' with 'what is permanent' (3:11). But sometimes there is an argument from the lesser to the greater – if 'the ministry of death' came with glory, 'will not the ministry of the Spirit have even more glory?' (3:7–8), and 'if there was glory in the ministry of condemnation, the ministry of righteousness must far exceed it in glory' (3:9).

The polarization between the two glories actually develops to the point where Paul can say, 'what once had glory has come to have no glory at all, because of the glory that surpasses it' (3:10). Just as the sun outshines the moon, so the glory of the New Covenant outshines the glory of the Old Covenant. Something of God's splendour could be experienced through the law but a greater experience comes through the gospel. Climactically, Paul contends that 'if what was being brought to an end came with glory, how much more will what is permanent have glory' (3:11).

Exodus 34:29–35 records that when Moses came down from Mount Sinai with the two tablets of the law in his hand, the skin of his face shone 'because he had been talking with God'. This phenomenon was experienced again when he went into the tent of meeting to speak with the Lord. Whenever he finished commanding the people what God had said to him, Moses put a veil over his face.

---

13. G. Kittel, *TDNT* 2:247–248, observes that in NT use of the noun *doxa* (glory) 'there is always expressed the divine mode of being, though with varying emphasis on the element of visibility'. The NT takes a decisive step by using in relation to Christ a word that in the OT was used in relation to God (e.g. Mark 13:26; John 2:11; Acts 7:55; 1 Pet. 1:21; 4:11; 2 Pet. 1:17).

Paul's gloss on this text is that the glory of God was reflected to the people *visually*, as Moses transmitted the words of God to them. But 'the Israelites could not gaze at Moses' face because of its glory, which was being brought to an end' (3:7, *katargoumenēn*).[14]

A similar expression is found in 3:11, where Paul says, 'if what was being brought to an end (*to katargoumenon*) came with glory, much more will what is permanent have glory'. Again, in 3:13 he says that Moses 'put a veil over his face so that the Israelites might not gaze at the outcome of what was being brought to an end' (*eis to telos tou katargoumenou*). These three expressions together suggest that Paul was attacking the view that the glory of Moses was undiminished.[15] Paul argued this way because his rivals taught that the law of Moses remained in force and was still the way to encounter God's splendour and be changed by it.

Speaking from the standpoint of New Covenant fulfilment, Paul argues that there was an end or goal for the law, which is Christ (cf. Rom. 10:4, *telos*). In fact, from the moment the law was given it was being 'brought to an end' by God himself. It had a limited life and was actually designed to point to Christ and his saving work (cf. Heb. 9:8–15, 24–28; 10:1–10).

In view of Paul's allusions in 4:1–6, Barnett suggests there is an autobiographical perspective to 3:7–18:

> The 'glory' of 'the ministry of the Spirit' is to be seen in [Paul]. As an
> Israelite he had been blinded to the glory on Moses' face. But now on

14. Older editions of the NIV render this verb 'fading', but the 2011 edition follows TNIV, 'transitory though it was'. A. T. Hanson, *Jesus Christ in the Old Testament* (London: SPCK, 1965), pp. 23–25, argues that it is best understood in terms of Paul's usage elsewhere (e.g. 1 Cor. 13:8, 10–11) to express the idea of something being invalidated or replaced. So ESV reads, 'which was being brought to an end' and NRSV, 'set aside'.

15. Martin, *2 Corinthians*, p. 62, records that this was the wording of the Jewish Targum Onqelos on Deut. 34:7. Martin, pp. 63–64, cites further Jewish tradition about the incident in Exod. 34. Blanton, 'Spirit and Covenant Renewal', pp. 145–147, rightly argues that 3:7–16 is bracketed by apologetic material and is polemical, not simply didactic.

the Damascus Road, having seen the glory to which Moses' glory
pointed, that is, toward the glorified Christ, and having turned to that
Lord, Paul has come to experience the blessings of freedom and life
through the Spirit.[16]

As a beneficiary of the New Covenant, made with 'the house of
Israel and the house of Judah' (Jer. 31:31), Paul was a renewed
Israelite. As such, he appealed to Jews to turn to Jesus as Messiah
and Lord and experience the same transformation. In line with
prophetic expectation he also called people from every nation to
share the blessings of the messianic era (cf. Isa. 2:2–3; 49:6; Jer. 3:17;
12:16; 16:19–21; Ezek. 37:26–28).[17] So he warns the Corinthians
about embracing the message of his rivals, which would lead to
condemnation and death. Those who had experienced the coming
of the Spirit through the preaching of the Son of God needed to
remember that all the promises of God find their 'Yes' in him
(1:18–20).

Revealing the glory of the Lord

The glory of the New Covenant is all the things previously noted
from the context: the Spirit who gives life instead of death, righteousness instead of condemnation, permanence instead of
transience. But the fundamental claim of the passage, arising from
the analogy with Moses in Exodus 34, is that the mediator of the
New Covenant reflects the glory of God to the people of God in
a transforming way. Paul goes on to identify Jesus as 'the image of
God', who brings 'the light of the knowledge of the glory of God'
(4:4–6). Remarkably, that glory continues to shine in 'the gospel of

---

16. Barnett, *Second Corinthians*, p. 184. S. Kim, *The Origin of Paul's Gospel* (Grand
    Rapids: Eerdmans, 1981), examines various allusions in Paul's letters to the
    Damascus Christophany and considers their implication for the apostle and
    his message.

17. In another piece of intertextual exegesis Paul writes that in Christ Jesus the
    blessing promised to Abraham (Gen. 12:2–3) has come upon the Gentiles,
    'so that we might receive the promised Spirit through faith' (Gal. 3:14).

the glory of Christ' (4:4), which Paul proclaims and models in his own ministry. By implication, authentic gospel ministry in every age will be the means by which the glory of Christ is revealed and believers are transformed.

Moses is said to have put a veil over his face in Exodus 34 to prevent the Israelites from seeing 'the outcome of what was being brought to an end' (3:13).[18] But Paul also suggests that Moses veiled his face because 'their minds were hardened' (3:14). Indeed, he observes that the same hardness towards God was evidenced in his day when 'the old covenant' was being read.[19] This echoes Jeremiah's claim that the Israelites 'did not obey or incline their ear, but everyone walked in the stubbornness of his evil heart' (Jer. 11:8; cf. 17:9–10). As a nation, they needed to be circumcised to the Lord in their hearts (Jer. 4:1–4; cf. 9:25–26; Deut. 10:16; 30:6). God promised to initiate a new covenant to make that possible.

Extending the image of the veil to his contemporaries, Paul relates it to their hardness of heart, saying 'that same veil remains unlifted, because only through Christ is it taken away' (3:14). What was *literally* veiled from the Israelites in Moses' day remained *figuratively* veiled to their descendants: 'their hardened minds were responsible for their blindness to the eschatological glory'.[20] 'Yes', Paul reiterates, 'to this day whenever Moses is read a veil lies over their hearts. But when one turns to the Lord, the veil is removed' (3:15–16).

Speaking representatively and contrasting his readers with unbelieving Israelites, Paul says 'we have such a hope', referring to the

---

18. A purpose clause (*pros to mē atenisai*) is used in 3:13 ('so that [the Israelites] might not gaze'), whereas a result clause is employed in 3:7 (*hōste mē dynasthai atenisai*, 'such [glory] that [the Israelites] could not gaze').

19. Paul alone in the NT uses the expression 'the old covenant', though Heb. 8:13 comes close. In 2 Cor. 3:15 the parallel expression is 'when Moses is read', suggesting that the Torah, or first five books of the Bible, are specifically in view. These were systematically read in Jewish synagogues (cf. Acts 13:15; 15:21).

20. Barnett, *Second Corinthians*, p. 193. Paul significantly uses the same verb to describe the abolition of the veil (3:14, *katargeitai*) as he does for the 'being-abolished glory' of the Old Covenant in vv. 7, 11, 13.

permanence and glory that the New Covenant brings (3:12). Although the apostle continues to focus on the character of his own God-given ministry, there is a broader reference to Christian experience here, as in 3:18 ('we all'). The autobiographical dimension to his argument (3:14 – 4:6) has already been noted. Paul was a 'veiled' Israelite, but the veil was removed when he met the glorified Lord Jesus. When Paul claims to be 'very bold' or 'very open' (3:12), he uses the word *parrēsia* as Hebrews does (3:6; 4:16; 10:19, 35) to describe the 'confidence' or 'openness' in relation to God that the New Covenant makes possible. This enables a confidence in gospel ministry for Paul (cf. 2 Cor. 7:14; Eph. 6:19; Phil. 1:20; Phlm. 8).[21]

In 3:16–18 the apostle explains what it means to be open or unveiled before the Lord. Not just Moses, but 'anyone' can come into God's presence with the veil removed. This happens when one turns to the Lord Jesus as Paul did (Acts 9:5–19). The phrase 'turn to the Lord', which is regularly used in the Old Testament for returning to the God of the covenant with penitence (e.g. Deut. 4:30; 2 Chr. 24:19; Isa. 19:22; Jer. 3:12, 14; 4:1–2), is employed in the New Testament to describe Christian conversion (e.g. 1 Thess. 1:9; Acts 9:35; 11:21; 14:15; 15:19; 26:20; 1 Pet. 2:25).

Bringing freedom

The claim that 'the Lord is the Spirit' (3:17) does not simply equate Jesus or God with the Spirit.[22] Elsewhere in the New Testament, the Lord Jesus is portrayed as the *giver* of the Spirit (cf. John 4:14; 7:37–39; 15:26; 16:7; Acts 2:33). The Spirit comes as people respond with repentance and faith to the message about Jesus as Lord and Christ (cf. Acts 2:36–39; 10:44; 19:2; Gal. 3:1–5; Eph. 1:13). Indeed,

---

21. Cf. Eph. 3:12; 1 Tim. 3:13. Note also Acts 2:29; 4:13, 29, 31; 28:31; 1 John 2:28; 3:21; 4:17; 5:14.

22. Fee, *God's Empowering Presence*, p. 311, n. 91, rightly argues that 'Paul is not trying to identify Christ with the Spirit; neither is he suggesting that the Spirit is in some way to be equated with the risen Christ.' Rather, this is an interpretative device whereby Paul keeps alive his argument that his ministry is that of 'the new covenant of Spirit'.

the Spirit is at work through the preaching of the gospel to make such a response possible. In effect, however, those who turn to the Lord turn to the Spirit, who is the key to ministry under the New Covenant.

> The Spirit, who applies the work of Christ to the life of the believer, is the key to the eschatological experience of God's presence. With the veil removed from the hardened heart, God's people enter into freedom.[23]

Paul clarifies his argument by adding 'and where the Spirit of the Lord is, there is freedom' (3:17). The expression 'the Spirit of the Lord' is unique in Paul's writings. It refers to the Spirit of God in various biblical texts (e.g. Judg. 3:10; 11:29; 1 Sam. 10:6; Isa. 61:1; Acts 8:39) and is equivalent to 'the Spirit of the living God' in 3:3. The term is used to avoid an absolute identification of the Spirit with Christ in 3:17. So a trinitarian view of God and his involvement in the process of salvation is indicated in this passage (cf. 13:14).

What is the freedom that the Spirit brings? Negatively, we may conclude from the preceding context that it is freedom from 'the ministry of death, carved in letters on stone', or freedom from the condemnation of the law and from obedience to the letter that kills. Positively, we may say from what follows that it is freedom to behold God's glory in Christ and to be transformed by it, because the veil is removed by the Spirit.[24] The transformation of Moses' face actually pointed forward to the change effected in the lives of all who turn to God in Christ and receive his life-giving Spirit.

Christian freedom is not a licence to sin, but a freedom to fulfil the essential demand of the law to love God and neighbour (cf. Mark 12:28–34; Rom. 13:8–10; Gal. 5:13–14; 6:2). It is a freedom

---

23. Ibid., p. 312.

24. Fee, ibid., p. 313, notes how the two parts of 3:17 together interpret the two sides of 3:16, making it clear that the Spirit removes the veil.

to serve God not under the old 'written code' but in the 'new way of the Spirit' (Rom. 7:6). Spirit-empowered and Spirit-directed freedom will not gratify the desires of the flesh but will manifest the 'fruit' that is pleasing to God (Gal. 5:16–26). Christians are not 'under the law' but live under the lordship of Christ (1 Cor. 9:20–21), who works through his Spirit to change them into his likeness.[25]

In 1 Thessalonians 4:9, where Paul says 'you yourselves have been *taught by God* to love one another', there is an interesting parallel to Jeremiah 31:33 (cf. Isa. 54:13; John 6:45). Of course, the apostle's own instruction and the teaching of Scripture have convinced them of the need for such love. But the preceding verse combines the notion of divine instruction through the apostle with the reminder that God has given his Holy Spirit to his people. God is at work in the people of the New Covenant through the energizing and consecrating power of his Spirit, teaching and moulding them through his implanted word to conform to his will (cf. 1 Cor. 2:13). So 'it is God's activity within the hearts of Christians that *impels* them to action'.[26] God's holiness – what he essentially is – is present to us in the Holy Spirit. God's Spirit demands and makes possible the reflection of his holiness in the lives of his people.

Bringing transformation

Every believer under the New Covenant 'sees' the glory of the Lord 'with unveiled face' (3:18). Like Moses, however, Christians do not yet behold God directly (cf. 1 Cor. 13:12). The next clause (*tēn doxan*

---

25. Cf. D. G. Peterson, 'Sanctification and God's Law', Appendix B in *Possessed by God: A New Testament Theology of Sanctification and Holiness*, NSBT 1 (Downers Grove: InterVarsity Press; Leicester: Apollos, 1995), pp. 143–149.

26. T. J. Deidun, *New Covenant Morality in Paul* (Rome: Pontifical Biblical Institute, 1981), p. 58. The Thessalonians' love for one another is 'the effect of God's immediate and efficacious action at the very source of their moral personality' (p. 58). In the holy people of the New Covenant, 'the consecrating and unifying power of God's presence is interiorised' (p. 60).

kyriou katoptrizomenoi) is best rendered 'seeing as in a mirror the glory of the Lord'. This expression allows Paul to 'postulate a real "seeing", yet one that in the present age falls short of actually seeing the Lord "face to face" as it were'.[27] This present knowledge of the Lord comes through 'the gospel of the glory of Christ, who is the image of God' (4:4; cf. Col. 1:15). So 'seeing' is actually a metaphor for 'hearing' the gospel of Christ (cf. Rom. 10:17; Gal. 3:1–5).

Significantly, Paul talks about God shining 'in our hearts' to give 'the light of the knowledge of the glory of God in the face of Jesus Christ' (4:6). Outwardly, Paul saw the glory of God when he met the risen Lord on the road to Damascus. At the same time, God shone inwardly in his heart to give the knowledge that transformed him (cf. Gal. 1:16). This made it possible for Paul to bring the light of the knowledge of God to others, by preaching Jesus Christ as Lord (4:5; cf. 2:14–16).[28] But it is clear from 3:18 that *all* who encounter the glory of Christ through the gospel can be changed. Moreover, if God has shone into our hearts, we too can be the means of that light being shared with others. Jeremiah's prediction that hearts would be changed and that all God's people would know him, 'from the least of them to the greatest' (Jer. 31:33–34) is thus fulfilled.

When Moses appealed for a confirmation of God's presence by asking to see a fuller revelation of his glory (Exod. 33:18), his request was answered with the promise of a theophany in which the Lord

---

27. Fee, *God's Empowering Presence*, p. 317. The participle *katoptrizomenoi* has been understood to mean 'behold as in a mirror (*katoptron*)' (NASB) or 'seeing [the glory of the Lord] as though reflected in a mirror' (NRSV). Some translations such as NIV ('reflect the Lord's glory'), TNIV ('contemplate the Lord's glory') and ESV ('behold the Lord's glory') omit any reference to a mirror. Fee, pp. 316–317, notes that although some evidence for the meaning 'reflect' can be found, the Greek verb normally means 'to look into a mirror' (so also BDAG).

28. In 4:1–6 Paul is speaking about the ministry of the New Covenant that he received 'by the mercy of God'. Although he consistently uses the first person plural in this passage, the reference is to his apostolate. So 4:6 means that God has shone into Paul's heart (lit. 'our hearts') to give the light of the knowledge of God to others.

would proclaim his *name*, parade his goodness before Moses, and reveal his graciousness (33:19–23). Although Moses could not see God's 'face', his glory would pass by and Moses would see God's 'back'. The true glory of God could not be penetrated, but God was pleased to reveal himself *in words* that could be understood and acknowledged by all his people.

God's extraordinary mercy and grace were expressed in the continuation of his covenant commitment, despite the rebellion of Israel. These truths were expressed when the Lord proclaimed his 'name' (34:6–7), which is another way of describing a revelation of his character. Even more wonderfully, Christians have seen the glory of God revealed in the person and work of the Lord Jesus Christ. Mercy and truth, grace and righteousness, love and holiness shine into our hearts from the Son of God.

The verb *metamorphoumetha* means 'to remodel' or 'to change into another form'.[29] Linked with the expression 'the same image' (*tēn autēn eikona*), this verb indicates that we are changed into the likeness of Christ, who is himself the true image of God. In Christ we see not only the radiance of God's glory but also the true image of humanity. Into that one image we are all being transformed *together* (cf. Rom. 8:29; 1 Cor. 15:49; Col. 3:10).[30]

The passive 'we are being transformed' emphasizes that this is the Spirit's work in us ('for this comes from the Lord who is the Spirit'). 'The One who is the *end* of our transformation ("the Lord") is also its means and provider (through "the Spirit").'[31]

---

29. J. Behm, *TDNT* 4:755. The same verb is used of the 'transfiguration' of Jesus in Mark 9:2; Matt. 17:2. What happened to Jesus was an anticipation and guarantee of the change promised to believers in the age to come.

30. The adjective 'same' (*autēn*) indicates that the goal of transformation is the same for all believers, namely, becoming like Christ, who is the image of God (4:4, *eikōn tou theou*). Cf. Eph. 4:24; 1 John 3:2. Fee, *God's Empowering Presence*, p. 318, considers alternative readings of the expression 'being transformed into the same image'.

31. Barnett, *Second Corinthians*, pp. 208–209. Paul's final claim in 3:18 takes us back to 3:17 ('now the Lord is the Spirit'), reaffirming that the Spirit is the key to our experience of God under the New Covenant.

Even though Paul uses a verb much employed in the Hellenistic mystery religions, there is a vast difference in the way he conceives transformation taking place. It is effected by God's Spirit, not by us. It is effected by gazing at Christ in the gospel, not by oft-repeated ritual or esoteric knowledge. 'Mystical deification finds no place; the change into the likeness of Christ (cf. also Rom. 8:29) is a re-attainment of the divine likeness of man at creation.'[32]

'From one degree of glory to another' (*apo doxēs eis doxan*) means from the present state of glory to the glory experienced when our bodies are redeemed (cf. Rom. 8:21, 23). This is more likely than the view that 'from glory' indicates the source of the transformation and 'to glory' its result at the time of the resurrection.[33] The present tense of the verb 'transform' suggests that the change is ongoing and progressive. But the disjunction between this age and the next must be kept in mind. Those who are alive at the time of Christ's return will experience complete and immediate transformation (cf. 1 Cor. 15:50–53; 1 Thess. 4:15–18). But ultimate glorification for those who have died will take place when their bodies are resurrected.

Paul wants us to hold these two truths together: we experience God's glory in the present, but there is a greater experience to come. We should not confuse the initial stage of spiritual life with its perfection in the future. The link between now and then is 'pneumatological or Christological rather than anthropological. It resides in the possession and activity of the Spirit, not in the

---

32. J. Behm, *TDNT* 4:758. Behm argues that Paul maintains 'the characteristically biblical distance between God and man'. Cf. Barnett, *Second Corinthians*, p. 207, n. 48.

33. G. Kittel, *TDNT* 2:250, observes that NT references to the participation of believers in glory are 'simply part of the general statement of salvation history concerning the connexion and parallelism between the resurrection of Christ and the resurrection and new aeon of believers'. Participation in glory, 'whether here in hope or one day in consummation, is participation in Christ'.

persistence of an immortal ego.'[34] Whatever change the Spirit effects in us now is only an anticipation of what is to come.

The Spirit's present work in us is a sign of the overlap of the ages and a pledge of ultimate transformation (2 Cor. 1:21–22; 5:5). As the element of continuity between this age and the next, the Holy Spirit prepares us for the climactic transformation that will mark the end of the process at the resurrection of the dead. But the picture is not a simple one of becoming more and more like Christ every day. Progress is rarely in a straight line, as we struggle with temptation and sin, persecution and suffering, decay and death (4:7–18; cf. Rom. 8:31–39). When change does not take place at the desired rate, Christians ought not to be bowed down with a sense of failure, but 'press on toward the goal for the prize of the upward call of God in Christ Jesus' (Phil. 3:14).

The reality is that 'we ourselves, who have the firstfruits of the Spirit, groan inwardly as we wait eagerly for adoption as sons, the redemption of our bodies' (Rom. 8:23; cf. 7:24–25). Spirit-filled Christian living cannot simply be equated with perfectionism or triumphalism. We groan together with the whole created order 'in the pains of childbirth' (Rom. 8:22), as we wait for God's new creation to be consummated. Even as we struggle to know what to pray, the Spirit helps us in our weakness, interceding for us 'with groanings too deep for words' (Rom. 8:26). Conformity to the likeness of Christ takes place in the context of suffering, weakness and testing, as we progress in faith, hope and love.

In short, there are two stages of the Spirit's work alluded to in 2 Corinthians 3:18. 'There is the ongoing present metamorphosis

---

34. M. J. Harris, *Raised Immortal: The Relation Between Resurrection and Immortality in New Testament Teaching* (London: Marshall, Morgan & Scott, 1983), p. 148. Harris argues that 'one and the same Spirit initiates and completes the spiritual and somatic transformation of believers and then sustains their resurrection life' (p. 148). Cf. J. M. Scott, *Adoption as Sons of God*, WUNT 2.48 (Tübingen: Mohr, 1992), pp. 256–266.

of character, and also the creation of the final "degree of glory" when Christians come to bear perfectly the image of the man from heaven (Rom. 8:29; 1 Cor. 15:49).'[35]

Justification and the Holy Spirit

The ministry of righteousness

Paul's rivals described themselves as 'ministers of righteousness' (11:15, *diakonoi dikaiosynēs*), apparently teaching that a New Covenant relationship with God makes it possible to find righteousness through keeping the law. But the apostle goes on to speak about their enslaving the Corinthians (11:20, *hymas katadouloi*), using a term he also employs in Galatians 2:4 in an argument against submission to law-keeping. Paul is certainly concerned to encourage the sort of behaviour that pleases God (6:7, 14). Furthermore, he teaches that God produces a 'harvest' of righteousness in those who are reconciled to him in Christ (9:9–10). But *the Spirit* produces this fruit, not believers seeking to obey the law of Moses.

As already noted, the newcomers to Corinth seem to have argued that the Mosaic Covenant was simply renewed in Christ, and that Christians are somehow bound to the letter of the law if they want to experience God's glory (3:7–11). They opposed Paul's preaching that the old dispensation had been fulfilled and replaced in Christ. The apostle's response was to describe the law as 'the ministry of death' and 'the ministry of condemnation' and to contrast it with 'the ministry of righteousness', which he says 'must far exceed it in glory' (3:9).

'Righteousness' (*dikaiosynē*) has been mentioned only once before in Paul's correspondence with the Corinthians, where Christ is said to have been made 'our righteousness' (1 Cor.

---

35. Harris, *Raised Immortal*, p. 149.

1:30).[36] The cognate verb is used in 1 Corinthians 6:11 (*edikaiōthēte*, 'you were justified') to describe the same benefits. Since 'righteousness' in 2 Corinthians 3:9 is contrasted with 'condemnation', it should be understood in a forensic way to refer to acquittal or vindication, the *status* attributed by God to those who trust in the saving work of his Son (cf. Gal. 5:5; Phil. 3:9). It is another way of talking about justification by faith, as preached by the apostle and embraced by the Corinthians. The term 'ministry of righteousness' (*diakonia tēs dikaiosynēs*, NRSV 'ministry of justification') is employed in 2 Corinthians 3:9 in response to the claim of Paul's rivals that *they* are 'ministers of righteousness' (11:15).

Paul's ministry of righteousness is later described as 'the ministry of reconciliation' (5:18), which involves proclaiming 'the message of reconciliation' entrusted to him (5:19). In essence, that message is about God reconciling the world to himself in Christ, 'not counting their trespasses against them'. There could be an echo of Jeremiah 31:34 here, suggesting that a new status of righteousness is made possible by the definitive forgiveness of sins. Paul restates his transformative message in 5:21 when he declares, 'for our sake he [God] made him to be sin who knew no sin, so that in him we might become the righteousness of God'.[37]

---

36. A. C. Thiselton, *The First Epistle to the Corinthians: A Commentary on the Greek Text*, NIGTC (Grand Rapids: Eerdmans; Carlisle: Paternoster, 2000), p. 191, argues that the four qualities mentioned in 1 Cor. 1:30 (wisdom, righteousness, sanctification, redemption) 'both characterize Christ and are imparted by Christ' (emphasis removed). The view of N. T. Wright, *Justification: God's Plan and Paul's Vision* (London: SPCK, 2009), p. 134, that those who are 'in Christ' share in the vindication of his resurrection does not sufficiently capture the forensic dimension to Paul's use of this terminology.

37. Wright, *Justification*, pp. 135–144, rightly argues that the entire section 2:14–6:13 is about Paul's servant ministry and the way it works out in practice, but reads the last clause of 5:21 as a reference to God's covenant faithfulness being embodied in apostolic ministry. It is more likely that Paul restates the 'message of reconciliation' he preaches, with its forensic basis (5:19, 'not counting their trespasses against them'), and adds the positive, salvific purpose of Christ being made sin for us ('so that in him we might become the righteousness of God').

The ministry of the Spirit

Paul describes the ministry of the Spirit in several ways in this chapter. The Spirit writes 'a letter from Christ' on the hearts of his people (3:3), the Spirit gives life instead of condemnation and death (3:6–7), the Spirit brings freedom to change (3:17), by transforming believers into the likeness of their Lord from one degree of glory to another (3:18). However, the parallel between 'the ministry of the Spirit' and 'the ministry of righteousness' in 3:9 suggests that the Spirit's fundamental work is to bring the certainty of sins forgiven and of reconciliation with God through the preaching of the gospel.[38] Justification brings life instead of death. Assured of the grace of God, believers are set free from condemnation and guilt to serve God and be transformed into the likeness of his Son.

In line with Jeremiah's predictions, Paul sees the need for reconciliation with God to be proclaimed, presenting a new knowledge of God and his grace and making possible a change of heart and direction. Using the language of Genesis 1, the apostle declares that 'God, who said ,"Let light shine out of darkness," has shone in our hearts to give the light of the knowledge of the glory of God in the face of Jesus Christ' (4:6). New creation language is later used to describe this transformation: 'if anyone is in Christ, the new creation has come: the old is gone, the new is here!' (5:17, TNIV). God's intention to renew humanity in the context of a new creation begins to be experienced by those who turn to Christ.

But the gospel is veiled to those who are perishing, because 'the god of this world has blinded the minds of the unbelievers, to keep them from seeing the light of the gospel of the glory of Christ, who is the image of God' (4:3–4). Only the proclamation of Jesus Christ as Lord (4:5) can dispel the darkness of ignorance, fear and guilt.

---

38. Fee, *God's Empowering Presence*, p. 308, says 'the "ministry of the Spirit" is also "the ministry of justification", that is, the ministry that has brought the experience of justification to them through the Spirit'. Cf. 1 Cor. 6:11; Gal. 5:5.

Yet God must 'shine' in the hearts of those who hear the gospel if the veil is to be removed (4:6). Only then can those who are perishing see and believe. Although Paul does not expressly say so, we are probably meant to understand that it is the Spirit who applies the message to hearts and minds, when it is proclaimed, to bring about the knowledge of God that transforms.[39]

As a minister of the New Covenant, Paul sees himself as one through whom the Spirit works. This happens as he is led through suffering and triumph to spread the fragrance of the knowledge of Christ everywhere (2:14). The Spirit works through Paul's teaching and proclamation, but also through the Christlike model he offers in the pattern of his ministry (cf. 4:7–15). His letters show that the gospel is not simply the means of bringing people to faith but also the means of nurturing believers and bringing them to maturity in Christ. Every problem he confronts is discussed in relation to the gospel. Every exhortation is grounded in the gospel and the world view he seeks to impart is determined by the gospel.

Paul's defence in 2 Corinthians is therefore a challenge to all who would share in the ministry of the New Covenant. It causes Paul not to 'lose heart' (4:1, 16), despite the suffering and persecution he endures (4:7–15), and despite the fact that his 'outer nature is wasting away' (4:16–18, my tr.; cf. 12:1–10). This ministry also involves a challenge to embrace the same ethical qualities as those stated by the apostle in 4:2:

> We have renounced disgraceful, underhanded ways. We refuse to practise cunning or to tamper with God's word, but by the open statement of the truth we would commend ourselves to everyone's conscience in the sight of God.

---

39. Fee, ibid., p. 321, argues that 'the Spirit lies close at hand in the language of "shining" and "enlightening"'. Fee, pp. 323–324, also argues from 4:13 that the life of faith is the gift of the Spirit: the Spirit not only gives life 'but also engenders the faith that causes one to receive the Spirit and thus enter into life'. Cf. Peterson, *Possessed by God*, pp. 60–62.

Conclusion

Against the insistence of his opponents that the glory of Moses and his covenant remain undiminished, Paul writes of the surpassing glory of the New Covenant, with its ministry of righteousness and of the Spirit of God (3:7–18). As one who has seen 'the glory of God in the face of Jesus Christ' (4:6), Paul has a God-given confidence and competence as a minister of the New Covenant (3:4–6), knowing that both the *content* and the *manner* of his ministry are the means by which God brings spiritual life and transformation to believers, wherever and however God leads him (2:14–17).

The presence and activity of the Spirit in the Corinthians, which is the result of his preaching to them (1:19–22), is the divine commendation of his ministry (3:1–3). As the beneficiaries of the New Covenant, Christians are free from the letter of the law to be transformed into the kind of people they were created to be, living as the image of God (3:17–18). What the law was seeking to achieve for Israel is now accomplished for believers in Christ through the ministry of the gospel by the enabling of the Spirit. Jeremiah's prophecy about the law being written on their heart and Ezekiel's co-ordinate promise of 'a new heart and a new spirit' are thus fulfilled.[40] This is experienced as the transforming knowledge of Christ spreads everywhere (2:14). Foundational to this knowledge is the certainty of justification by faith and of trespasses not being counted against those who believe.

Jeremiah's prophecy of the New Covenant provides a theological structure and basis to much of Paul's argument in 2 Corinthians 3 – 5. The apostle does not simply allude to key elements in that prophecy, but reveals how its promises are interconnected and fulfilled in Christ. Paul is driven by the inner logic of Jeremiah's oracle. At the same time, viewing that prophecy in the light of Ezekiel's predictions, Paul indicates that it is expressly by the Spirit

---

40. Barnett, *Second Corinthians*, pp. 46–47, also draws attention to the influence of Isa. 40 – 55 on what Paul writes in 2 Corinthians.

that 'we not only come to know God, but come to live in his Presence in such a way as constantly to be renewed into God's image'.[41]

The atoning work of Jesus provides a new experience of the grace of God that transforms hearts and minds through the enabling of the Spirit. Drawn to Jesus as Saviour and Lord, believers continue to gaze at the glory of God in the one who is the true image of God and to be changed into his likeness. The blessing of the New Covenant is thus not a new ability and desire to keep the law of Moses but an empowerment and direction to live for Christ and reflect his glory.

Pastorally, Paul's teaching about the ministry of the New Covenant highlights the need for transformation in three ways. First, there is the transformation of conversion to Christ, effected by the preaching of the gospel and the removal of the veil over human hearts by the work of the Spirit. The miraculous nature of this change is highlighted by Paul's New Creation theology.

Secondly, there is the ongoing character change effected by the Spirit, as believers continue to gaze at Christ and desire to share his image and glory. This transformation may not simply be progressive, because of the spiritual battle in which we are engaged and because of our waywardness and weakness. But present signs of transformation point to the ultimate experience of glorification that awaits us at the resurrection.

Thirdly, Paul's emphasis on Christians being transformed together (3:18; cf. Eph. 4:13), not in isolation or on different trajectories, finds its ultimate expression in the resurrection to eternal life. It is natural to be individualistic and to focus on one's own progress and growth. But the apostle addresses the Corinthians collectively. He urges them not to receive the grace of God in vain, but to widen their hearts towards him and respond to the ministry he brings in person and by letter (6:1–13). There are moral and relational issues that they must deal with to bring 'holiness to completion in the fear of God' (6:14 – 7:1). The rest of the letter is full of warnings and

---

41. Fee, *God's Empowering Presence*, p. 319.

encouragements that arise from Paul's exposition of the gospel and its implications for them.

Fundamentally, the apostle sees the need to point believers away from alternatives to the glory of Christ, who is the image of God. This is the essential task of New Covenant ministry, both with respect to evangelism and for the continuing nurture of the body of Christ, wherever it might be manifested.

Effective pastoral ministry will continually confront people with the reality of God's character and his provision for us in the person and work of the Lord Jesus. Like the apostle Paul, authentic ministers of the New Covenant will not make themselves the focus of attention but proclaim 'Jesus Christ as Lord, with ourselves as your servants for Jesus' sake' (4:5). Moreover, they will expose distortions of the gospel that obscure the glory of Christ and fail to bring the promised transformation.

Under the New Covenant, the *motivation* for change is the grace of God in the saving work of Jesus the Messiah, the Son of God. The *pattern* for change is the character, the life and the teaching of Jesus. The *empowerment* for change is the gift of the Holy Spirit. With this trinitarian focus, New Covenant ministry offers something radically new, enabling a transformation of believers collectively 'from one degree of glory to another'.

5. HEARTS AND LIVES TRANSFORMED

Apart from explicit mention of the New Covenant in the Corinthian letters (1 Cor. 11:25; 2 Cor. 3:6), the apostle Paul proclaims the fulfilment of similar expectations in at least two other significant contexts (Rom. 11:26–27; Gal. 4:24–28).[1] In these passages he conflates New Covenant promises from a range of prophetic oracles. Elsewhere in his writings he develops a New Covenant theology by employing words and themes associated with particular New Covenant promises.[2]

---

1. Rom. 9:4 could also include the New Covenant among 'the covenants' belonging to Israel (cf. Eph. 2:12, 'the covenants of promise').

2. Since the publication of E. P. Sanders, *Paul and Palestinian Judaism: A Comparison of Patterns of Religion* (London: SCM, 1977), many scholars have reconsidered the broader significance of covenant in Pauline theology. P. R. Williamson, *Sealed with an Oath: Covenant in God's Unfolding Purpose*, NSBT 23 (Downers Grove: InterVarsity Press; Nottingham: Apollos, 2007), pp. 186–188, outlines some significant arguments against the approach taken by Sanders.

Most importantly, he identifies the heart as the object of change and celebrates the transformation of behaviour that results from God's redemptive work. Paul uses heart language extensively, but I will focus on its application in his letter to the Romans. There he points to the reality of the law written on the heart of believers and explores what this means for those who are in Christ. Galatians 4:24–28 highlights the Spirit's role in this transformation.

Deliverance, justification and the Holy Spirit

Deliverance for Israel

In Romans 11:25–27 Paul deals with the problem that 'a partial hardening has come upon Israel'. Given the argument to this point, he does not imply that every Israelite without exception will be saved, but indicates that 'Israel would one day experience a spiritual rejuvenation that would extend far beyond the present bounds of the remnant.'[3] Surprisingly, however, this will not happen 'until the fullness of the Gentiles has come in'. Isaiah 59:20 is then conflated with phrases from other texts to guarantee and explain how 'all Israel will be saved':

> the Deliverer will come from Zion,
>> he will banish ungodliness from Jacob;
> and this will be my covenant with them
>> when I take away their sins.

Isaiah 59:20 in Hebrew reads 'to Zion', while the LXX reads 'for the sake of Zion' (*heneken Siōn*), but Paul has 'from Zion' (*ek Siōn*). Many commentators suggest that this change points to the final deliverance of Israel that will be accomplished by Christ when he

---

3. D. J. Moo, *The Epistle to the Romans*, NICNT (Grand Rapids: Eerdmans, 1996), p. 718. Moo, pp. 719–726, considers the different ways in which the clause 'and in this way all Israel will be saved' has been understood.

comes from the heavenly Jerusalem.[4] Paul then follows the LXX ('he will banish ungodliness from Jacob'), rather than the Hebrew ('to those in Jacob who turn from transgression'), to highlight the gracious act of God in delivering his people from their unbelief and disobedience. However, taking this text as a specific reference to the work of the returning Messiah is odd.

Although the heavenly Jerusalem is mentioned in Galatians 4:26 (cf. Heb. 12:22; Rev. 3:12; 21:2), 'Zion' and 'Jacob' are literary variants for 'Israel' in Isaiah 59:20 and should be understood that way in Romans 11:26. Paul modified the text to read 'from Zion' because he wanted to stress that the Messiah would arise from the midst of God's holy people.[5] Romans 1 – 8 implies that the promises of the New Covenant have already been fulfilled through the coming of the Messiah to Israel. The blessings are available for anyone who believes the gospel, Jew or Gentile (1:16–17; 3:21–31; 4:1–25). As in 2 Corinthians 3, the apostle makes it clear that these benefits are spread abroad through his own ministry (cf. Rom. 1:8–15; 15:15–33).

Even though many Israelites remain hardened to the gospel, Paul does not waver in his desire for them to inherit what God promised them (9:1–5; 10:1). He even sees his ministry of preaching to Gentiles as a way of making fellow Jews jealous and thus saving some of them (11:13–14). So Paul is not talking about a sudden turning to Christ by Jews at the second coming but about a process

---

4. Cf. C. E. B. Cranfield, *The Epistle to the Romans*, vol. 2, ICC (Edinburgh: T. & T. Clark, 1979), pp. 577–578; T. R. Schreiner, *Romans*, BECNT (Grand Rapids: Baker Academic, 1998), pp. 619–623; Moo, *Romans*, p. 728.

5. J. Fitzmyer, *Romans*, AB 33 (New York: Doubleday, 1993), p. 625, suggests that 'from Zion' may refer to 'Jesus' descent from David, or more generically, his origin from among the chosen Jewish people of old (cf. 9:5); or even to Jerusalem as the place of Christ's death and resurrection'. There is no mention of the second coming elsewhere in Rom. 9 – 11, and the verb 'will come' (Isa. 59:20) refers to the coming of the Messiah as a future event from the prophet's point in time.

that continues in the present and reaches its climax when Christ returns.[6]

The words 'this will be my covenant with them' are taken from Isaiah 59:21, which goes on to speak about God putting his Spirit upon them and placing his words in their mouth (cf. Joel 2:28–29). Adding the words 'when I take away their sins' in a slightly altered form from Isaiah 27:9, Paul indicates that he is thinking in terms of New Covenant fulfilment. This addition implies that Israel's deliverance can take place only by 'acceptance of the gospel message about the forgiveness of sins in Jesus Christ'.[7]

Read together, Isaiah 59:20 and 21 reflect the expectation that God will fulfil his covenant with Abraham by overcoming the hardness of Israelite hearts and giving his Spirit to them (cf. Ezek. 36:25–27). Addition of the words 'when I take away their sins' brings Paul's citation more closely in line with the specific predictions of Jeremiah 31:31–34.[8] Paul adapts Isaiah's prediction to express more emphatically the sequence of thought in Jeremiah's oracle: God will 'banish ungodliness from Jacob' when he takes away their sins. Since the death of Christ has achieved the promised redemption (Rom. 3:21–26) and made possible a definitive forgiveness of sins (4:5–8), what is needed now is a softening of hearts to believe this message and confess Jesus as Lord (10:8–13).

In short, then, Isaiah 59:20–21 is modified to make the point that the benefits of the New Covenant already achieved by Christ will most certainly be experienced by the full number of the elect in Israel (cf. 'fullness' in 11:12 and 11:25), even though some remain hardened for the moment against the gospel.

---

6. Cf. A. J. Köstenberger and P. T. O'Brien, *Salvation to the Ends of the Earth: A Biblical Theology of Mission*, NSBT 11 (Leicester: Apollos; Downers Grove: InterVarsity Press, 2001), pp. 190–191.

7. Moo, *Romans*, p. 729. Moo, pp. 725–726, critiques the view that Israel will be saved in a special way, particularly opposing suggestions of a different covenantal theology for Jews and Gentiles.

8. So Cranfield, *Romans*, vol. 2, pp. 578–579, and Schreiner, *Romans*, p. 620, n. 24, against Moo, *Romans*, p. 728.

Two covenants and their effect

In Galatians 4:24–25 Paul identifies 'two covenants' in his allegory about Hagar and Sarah. The first covenant is 'from Mount Sinai, bearing children for slavery'. The giving of the law to Israel is viewed in terms of what Genesis 16 says about the birth of Ishmael:

> just as the children of a slave-wife (unless acknowledged as true children by the husband and master) were destined to be slaves themselves, so the covenant of law given at Sinai committed all who embraced it to its binding power.[9]

Paul's opponents could well have argued that *Jews* are the children of Sarah the free woman, and *Gentiles* the children of Hagar the slave woman: Jews have been blessed with the law, while Gentiles are slaves to ignorance and sin. But in Paul's analogy, Hagar is the mother of 'the present Jerusalem', or Israel under the law, 'for she is in slavery with her children'. Sarah is the mother of Jews and Gentiles who belong to 'the Jerusalem above' (4:26), who are 'born according to the Spirit' (4:29), and are free from the law. If, as seems likely, Paul's opponents used Genesis 16 to support *their* case, 'Paul felt obliged to refute their argument by inverting it and showing that the incident, properly understood, supported the gospel of free grace, with its antithesis between flesh and spirit.'[10]

The second covenant is associated with freedom and being 'born according to the Spirit' (4:26–29). 'Paul takes it as self-evident that a straight line runs through Sarah and Isaac, the covenant of faith (because it depends on promise), the Jerusalem above (v. 26), and Christians.'[11] Isaiah 54:1 is used to proclaim that the new or heavenly

---

9. R. Y. K. Fung, *The Epistle to the Galatians*, NICNT (Grand Rapids: Eerdmans, 1988), pp. 206–207.

10. F. F. Bruce, *The Epistle to the Galatians: A Commentary on the Greek Text*, NIGTC (Exeter: Paternoster, 1982), p. 218. Bruce notes that the contrast between legal bondage and spiritual freedom here is identical with the contrast between law and Spirit in 2 Cor. 3.

11. Fung, *Galatians*, p. 207.

Jerusalem already has many citizens, who are 'children of promise' (cf. Heb. 12:22–24).

It is clear from Galatians 3:7–9 that Paul includes believing Jews and Gentiles among the children of promise (cf. Rom. 9:6–33; 11:1–24).[12] His predominantly Gentile readers are children of Abraham, who have experienced the fulfilment of what was promised by God: they are justified by faith, not by 'works of the law', and have received the Spirit through faith (3:1–14). Paul's point in using Isaiah 54:1 is that

> formerly the Gentiles were spiritually sterile, producing no fruit for God, but now their response to the gospel has made them more fruitful than the synagogue: the new Jerusalem has more children than the old Jerusalem ever did.[13]

So the second covenant is the Abrahamic one (cf. 3:17), interpreted and explained in terms of its fulfilment in Christ. It has been argued that

> what Paul describes as two covenants for the purposes of his exegesis are in effect two ways of understanding the one covenant purpose of God through Abraham and for his seed. What Paul is about to argue is that the Abrahamic covenant seen in terms of freedom and promise is a fuller expression of God's electing grace and a fuller embodiment of the ongoing divine will than the Abraham covenant seen in terms of law and flesh.[14]

That may be true, but Paul is still happy to speak of the covenant

---

12. Williamson, *Sealed with an Oath*, 192, says 'the covenant promises had been inherited not by Israel in an exclusively ethnic or biological sense, but by all Abraham's true descendants – those united to Abraham through faith in Jesus Christ'.

13. Bruce, *Galatians*, p. 222.

14. J. D. G. Dunn, *A Commentary on the Epistle to the Galatians*, BNTC (London: Black, 1993), p. 249.

made with Israel at Sinai (4:24; cf. 2 Cor. 3:14, 'the old covenant'), just as the Old Testament does (e.g. Exod. 24:7–8; 34:10).

For Paul, law and promise are antithetical.

> The law, which was given later, was a parenthetical dispensation introduced by God for a limited purpose; its validity continued only until the promise to Abraham was fulfilled in Christ, and even while it was valid it did not modify the terms of the promise (cf. 3:17–25).[15]

Spirit is paralleled with promise in 4:28–29, suggesting that the promise to Abraham is ultimately fulfilled in the giving of the Spirit (cf. 3:14).

Although Paul does not mention it by name in Galatians, the blessing of the New Covenant is the twofold gift of righteousness or justification by faith and the Holy Spirit (cf. 2 Cor. 3:8). Christians are not 'under the law' (Gal. 5:18), but faith in Christ 'working through love' (5:6) makes it possible for them to serve one another in love and so fulfil 'the whole law' (5:13–14).[16] Put another way, those who 'walk by the Spirit' will not gratify the desires of the flesh, but will manifest the fruit that the Spirit produces (5:16–26). So faith in the crucified Messiah makes possible a new life that issues in love (2:19 – 3:1), and hearing the gospel with faith makes possible the reception of the transforming Spirit (3:2–6).

The expression 'born according to the Spirit' (4:29) is the closest parallel in Paul's writings to John 3:6, 8, though Titus 3:5 speaks of 'the washing of regeneration and renewal of the Holy Spirit'. In the immediate context, 'Isaac represents those born through the power of the divine promise . . . which is another way of saying through

---

15. Bruce, *Galatians*, p. 219.
16. In an extended note on law and Christian living, B. Witherington III, *Grace in Galatia: A Commentary of St. Paul's Letter to the Galatians* (Edinburgh: T. & T. Clark, 1998), p. 342, argues that the Christian community is to be 'cruciform and Christological in shape. It is to follow his example and walk in and by the Spirit. It is, in short, to follow the Law of Christ, which is not identical with the Law of Moses.'

the power of God's Spirit.'[17] The emphasis in 3:2–6 is on reception
of the Spirit through hearing with faith, but 4:28–29 implies that
those who believe have been 'wrought upon by the Spirit of God'.[18]
The word of promise enables faith by the power of the Spirit,
and the Spirit continues to renew and transform those who believe
the gospel.

Renewal from within

In Paul's writings, the word 'heart' (*kardia*) is used in much the same
way as 'mind' (*nous*). As in the Old Testament, the heart denotes
the centre of the person as a rational, emotional and volitional
being. *Nous* is a more Hellenistic term, which in Paul's usage refers
to 'the rational person, the perceiving, thinking, determining "I",
the "I" not simply at the mercy of outside powers but able to
respond and to act with understanding'.[19] So in Romans Paul
moves from considering the effect of 'a debased mind' (1:28) to
speak of the mind being renewed (12:2), suggesting that 'the continuing work of mind-renewal . . . is at the heart of God's New
Covenant work'.[20]

Paul's employment of 'heart' language incorporates the emotive
dimension, as well as thinking and willing (e.g. Rom. 5:5; 9:2; 10:1).
Since God 'searches the heart' (8:27), the law and circumcision must
affect the heart (2:15, 29), and obedience and belief must be 'from
the heart' (6:17; 10:9–10). With such concerns he reflects New

---

17. Dunn, *Galatians*, p. 257. Witherington, *Grace in Galatia*, p. 336, suggests that
    'Paul wished to stress that the Galatians came to receive the promise and
    the inheritance in the same miraculous fashion as Isaac had – by divine
    intervention.'

18. Dunn, *Galatians*, p. 257.

19. J. D. G. Dunn, *The Theology of Paul the Apostle* (Edinburgh: T. & T. Clark,
    1998), p. 74. In Romans the word 'heart' is used fifteen times and the word
    'mind' six times.

20. Moo, *Romans*, p. 758.

Covenant expectations, insisting that 'the experience of God's grace penetrated to the innermost depths of a person and that the corresponding faith was an expression of deeply felt commitment'.[21]

Corrupted minds and hearts

Paul's indictment of sinful humanity in Romans 1:18–32 begins with the assertion that ungodly and unrighteous behaviour arises from suppressing the truth about God. In 2:18–20 he acknowledges that Israel was the beneficiary of special revelation, but here affirms that there is a knowledge of God available to humanity in general through his works of creation and providence. 'For what can be known about God is plain to them, because God has shown it to them.' Indeed, his invisible attributes, 'namely his eternal power and divine nature', have been clearly perceived in his handiwork ever since he created it (cf. Ps. 19:1–4). However, human beings are 'without excuse', 'for although they knew God, they did not honour him as God or give thanks to him, but they became futile in their thinking and their foolish hearts were darkened'.[22]

The description of 'hearts' as 'foolish' (1:21) suggests that it is 'the intellectual element in their inner lives which here is particularly in mind'.[23] Despite their claims to be wise, human beings show themselves to be fools when they fail to recognize and glorify the true God. But the problem is not simply intellectual. Paul goes on to speak of those who 'did not see fit to acknowledge God' (1:28, *ouk edokimasan ton theon echein en epignōsei*). They refuse to take God into account in making decisions and living their lives. God's response is to abandon them 'to a debased mind (*adokimon noun*), to

---

21. Dunn, *Theology of Paul*, p. 75.

22. Moo, *Romans*, pp. 106–107, discusses the limited nature of this knowledge and concludes that 'at the very center of every person, where the knowledge of God, if it is to have any positive effects, must be embraced, there has settled a darkness – a darkness that only the light of the gospel can penetrate'.

23. C. E. B. Cranfield, *The Epistle to the Romans*, vol. 1, ICC (Edinburgh: T. & T. Clark, 1975), p. 118.

do what ought not to be done'.[24] A list of vices follows (1:29–31), showing the practical consequences of choosing not to know God. Paul's final statement about the knowledge of God in 1:32 assumes the possibility of being aware of his righteousness 'and of his uncompromising hostility to evil, and therefore of the ultimate penalty of their evil-doing',[25] and yet not acting upon that knowledge.

A particular manifestation of human foolishness is the practice of idolatry (1:22–23), exchanging the truth about God for a lie and worshipping and serving created things, rather than the one who created them (1:25). Although some commentators have argued that this passage speaks only of the pagan world, 1:23 echoes the description of Israel's idolatry in Psalm 106:20 and Jeremiah 2:11. Furthermore, 2:21–23 accuses Jews of doing some of the very things outlined here. It would seem, therefore, that in 1:18–32 Paul is indicting pagan idolatry and the behaviour that flows from it in terms that undermine any sense of Jewish superiority, before he makes a more direct assault on it in Romans 2.[26]

The work of the law written on the heart

Paul's analysis of the human heart continues in Romans 2:1–5, where he addresses those who pass judgment on the behaviour outlined in 1:18–32, but do the very same things themselves. Such people think they will escape the judgment of God and 'presume on the riches of his kindness and forbearance and patience, not knowing that God's

---

24. There is a play on words in the Greek here: people who 'did not see fit' (*ouk edokimasan*) to retain the knowledge of God are handed over by God to 'an unfit mind' (*adokimon noun*), which leads to behaviour that is against the will of God. Cf. 1:24, 26.

25. Cranfield, *Romans*, vol. 1, p. 134. Paul speaks of 'what all people, whether blessed with special revelation or not, can know of God's just judgment' (Moo, *Romans*, p. 121).

26. N. T. Wright, 'Romans', in *NIB* 10 (2002), pp. 393–770 (433), observes that 'Paul's surface text describes paganism, but the subtext quietly includes Israel in the indictment.' Moo, *Romans*, pp. 109–110, argues that 'in a somewhat idealized, paradigmatic fashion' Paul describes 'the terrible proclivity of all people to corrupt the knowledge of God they possess by making gods of their own'.

kindness is meant to lead you to repentance'. Paul sees this lack of
repentance as evidence of a 'hard and impenitent heart' (cf. Deut.
10:16; Jer. 4:4), and warns that they are 'storing up wrath' for themselves
on the day of wrath, 'when God's righteous judgment will be revealed'.

In Romans 2 Paul argues with Jews who are confident about their
covenant status, believing they are right with God, and seeing no
need to turn to Christ.[27] He insists that the judgment of God will
come upon *all* who are 'self-seeking and do not obey the truth, but
obey unrighteousness', and insists that this judgment will be for 'the
Jew first and also the Greek' (2:8–9; cf. 10:16–21). So, in the final
analysis, he sees no difference between Jew and Gentile when it
comes to the need for God's mercy in Christ.

In 2:12–13 the apostle continues his argument about the judgment
of God falling on Jews and Gentiles alike: 'all who have sinned
without the law will also perish without the law, and all who have
sinned under the law will be judged by the law'. Although Jews distinguished themselves from Gentiles on the basis that they possessed
the law (2:17–20), Paul argues that 'it is not the hearers of the law
who are righteous before God, but the doers of the law who will be
justified' (cf. Matt. 7:24–27; 12:50; Jas 1:22–25). A true hearing of the
law involves heeding and obeying it, as many biblical texts indicate
(e.g. Exod. 15:26; Deut. 6:4–9; Jer. 11:3; 12:17). Those who are merely
hearers are not righteous in God's sight. Indeed, 'like his fellow Jews
and the whole prophetic tradition, Paul is ready to insist that a doing
of the law is necessary for final acquittal before God'.[28]

---

27. Cranfield, *Romans*, vol. 1, pp. 138–139; J. D. G. Dunn, *Romans 1–8*, WBC 38A
     (Dallas: Word, 1988), pp. 89–90; Moo, *Romans*, pp. 128–129.
28. Dunn, *Romans 1–8*, p. 98. Rom. 2:13 has aroused much discussion because it
     appears to be in conflict with Paul's later emphasis on justification by faith
     as a present reality, 'apart from works of the law' (3:21–24, 28; 5:1). Moo,
     Romans, p. 148, argues that 'this verse confirms and explains the reason for
     the Jews' condemnation in v. 12b; and this suggests that its purpose is not to
     show how people can be justified but to set forth the standard that must be
     met if a person is to be justified'. But Schreiner, *Romans*, p. 115, contends that
     'Paul's insistence elsewhere that works are necessary to enter the kingdom
     suggests that the similar theme here cannot be dismissed as hypothetical.'

As Paul continues to challenge Jewish unbelief and hypocrisy, he draws attention to the fact that Gentiles who do not have the law of Moses 'by nature' may 'do what the law requires', demonstrating that they are 'a law to themselves, even though they do not have the law' (2:14). In so doing, 'they show that the work of the law is written on their hearts' (2:15).

Many take these verses to mean that certain Gentiles, apart from special revelation, 'by nature do what the law requires'. In effect, 'they have the moral norms of the Mosaic law, evidenced by occasionally keeping the commandments of that law'.[29] These Gentiles 'possess the law' in the sense that it is written on their hearts and attested by their conscience (2:15–16). Paul is said to have borrowed the popular Greek conception of a natural law written on the heart and coupled this with another stereotypical Greek expression, 'they are a law to themselves'.[30] Gentiles will be judged on the basis of natural law, whereas Jews will be judged on the basis of the law given to Moses.

However, there are several reasons for believing that Paul specifically draws attention to Gentile Christians here, identifying them as those who enjoy the transformation predicted in connection with the promised New Covenant. They have the knowledge of God's will inscribed in their hearts and embody the teaching of the law in their actions.[31]

First, the expression 'by nature' (*physei*) is best read as modifying the preceding verb, so that the meaning is 'they do not have the law

29. Schreiner, *Romans*, p. 122. Schreiner, p. 124, takes Paul's language in 2:16 to imply that 'the doing of the law described in verse 14 should not be understood as a consistent and regular observance of the law'. Dunn, *Romans 1–8*, pp. 98–99, argues that this knowledge of rightness and wrongness by 'the godly pagan' has already been hinted at in 1:26–28.

30. Moo, *Romans*, p. 150, says Paul presses into service 'a widespread Greek tradition to the effect that all human beings possess an "unwritten" or "natural" law – an innate moral sense of "right and wrong"'.

31. S. J. Gathercole, 'A Law unto Themselves: The Gentiles in Romans 2:14–15 Revisited', *JSNT* 85 (2002), pp. 27–49 (37), takes the expression 'they are a law to themselves' to mean that 'these Gentiles incarnate the Torah in their persons'.

by nature', meaning 'by virtue of their birth'.[32] This removes the need to speculate about unbelieving Gentiles having a natural law written on the heart. Jews have the law as their natural inheritance; Gentiles do not.

Secondly, the expression 'the work of the law is written on their hearts' most obviously alludes to Jeremiah 31:33 (LXX 38:33). Elsewhere, Paul uses the plural expression 'works of the law' in a negative way (3:20, 28; Gal. 2:16; 3:2, 5, 10), but the singular expression 'the work of the law' (*to ergon tou nomou*) denotes something commendable,[33] and brings out 'the essential unity of the law's requirements'.[34] Those who take the natural law approach to Romans 2:14–16 either deny that this is an allusion to Jeremiah's prophecy or take Paul's expression to be 'a more open-ended formula, which has at least the potential of wider application'.[35]

In 2 Corinthians 3:2–3, 6 Paul modifies Jeremiah's promise about God writing his law upon the heart of his people and combines this with Ezekiel's promise of the renewing work of the Spirit. Given the eschatological significance of the promise in Jeremiah 31:33, it is hard to believe that Paul used the expression 'the work of the law is written on their hearts' in Romans 2:15 simply to refer to a fact of everyday life among the Gentiles. Even more odd is the

---

32. Cranfield, *Romans*, vol. 1, pp. 156–157. Cf. Schreiner, *Romans*, p. 121. Gathercole, 'Law unto Themselves', pp. 35–37, offers some significant grammatical reasons for linking this adverbial construction with the verb that precedes it. He also notes that *physei* in Paul's writings normally qualifies *identity*, rather than *behaviour*.

33. Dunn, *Romans 1–8*, says, 'what makes it commendable, and, in Paul's mind, marks it off from the plural phrase, is that this work of the law happens "in the heart"'.

34. Cranfield, *Romans*, vol. 1, p. 158. Cf. Rom. 8:4, 'the righteous requirement of the law' (*to dikaiōma tou nomou*), fulfilled in those who walk 'not according to the flesh but according to the Spirit'.

35. Dunn, *Romans 1–8*, p. 100. Dunn is prepared to admit that Jer. 31:33 is probably evoked in Rom. 2:15, but says it is deliberately modified to have a wider application. Gathercole, 'Law unto Themselves', p. 41, observes four specific verbal links between Jer. 38:33 (LXX) and Rom. 2:15.

suggestion that he borrowed a stereotypical Greek expression that was similar to Jeremiah's promise, but conveyed a different meaning, and used it at the beginning of a letter that regularly alludes to the fulfilment of Jeremiah's promise in other ways (cf. 2:26–29; 5:5; 6:17; 7:4–6; 8:4; 10:9–13; 11:26; 12:2)![36]

The third reason for taking Romans 2:14–16 as a reference to Gentile Christians concerns the flow of the argument in this chapter. Paul seeks to undermine Jewish self-confidence, based on the possession of the Mosaic law and circumcision. Part of his indictment is the reference to Gentile Christians enjoying the covenant blessings promised to Israel. They have been transformed by a remarkable work of God. Three expressions mark a decisive change from the description of Gentiles in the previous chapter: 'the work of the law is written on their hearts', their conscience bearing witness, and their 'conflicting thoughts' accusing or even excusing them on the Day of Judgment. Each of these witnesses is internal and together constitute 'features of a Christian believer'.[37]

Conscience appears to be a present, accompanying witness (*symmartyrousēs*) to 'the law is written on their hearts'. The closest parallel is Romans 9:1, where Paul claims that the Holy Spirit testifies through his conscience that he is speaking the truth in Christ and not lying. Although some commentators take 'their conflicting thoughts' to be a further description of the role of conscience, 'it is not the moral quality of the thoughts, but their forensic function on the day of judgment which is in view here'.[38] The 'showing'

---

36. Cf. N. T. Wright, 'The Law in Romans 2', in J. D. G. Dunn (ed.), *Paul and the Mosaic Law*, WUNT 89 (Tübingen: Mohr Siebeck, 1996), pp. 131–150 (147).

37. Gathercole, 'Law unto Themselves', p. 30. Gathercole, pp. 40–47, shows how each of these terms points to the work of God in believing Gentiles.

38. Ibid., p. 46. Gathercole, p. 45, observes that a Christian could have copious 'accusing thoughts' and still be vindicated by God (cf. 1 John 3:20). Condemnation of Gentiles on the basis of their wrong thinking is highlighted in 1:20–21, but in 2:15–16 even 'conflicting thoughts' can be a testimony to the Spirit's transforming work.

(*endeixis*) of these witnesses together is on that day, and inner transformation is the true object of God's judgment.

Circumcision of the heart

In Romans 2:15, then, 'we see a wonderful transformation from the natural state of the Gentile heart in Jewish perspective to a new heart, inscribed with the work of Torah'.[39] Consistent with the missionary strategy revealed in 11:14 – to provoke unbelieving Jews to jealousy and 'thus save some of them' – Paul points to the effect of the New Covenant on Gentile Christians to show why Jews need to turn to Christ. He continues to do this in the rest of Romans 2, where the parallels between 2:14–15 and 2:25–29 are particularly striking.

Once again, the apostle argues that possession of the law, even knowing God's will and approving what is excellent on the basis of instruction from the law, is of value only if you obey the law (2:17–24; cf. 2:13). This argument is specifically applied to circumcision, when Paul says 'circumcision indeed is of value if you obey the law, but if you break the law, your circumcision becomes uncircumcision' (2:25).[40] Circumcision does not guarantee salvation and will not protect disobedient Jews from God's wrath.

Provocatively, Paul then imagines the possibility of an uncircumcised Gentile keeping the precepts of the law and asks, 'will not his uncircumcision be regarded as circumcision?' (2:26; cf. 2:14) Such a person would embody what it meant to be a true Israelite and would be 'reckoned' by God (*logisthēsetai*; cf. 3:28; 4:3–6) to be a member of the covenant people. A physically uncircumcised man who kept the law would condemn those Jews who 'have the written code and circumcision but break the law' (2:27).

---

39. Ibid., p. 43.

40. Cranfield, *Romans*, vol. 1, p. 172, takes 2:25 to mean, 'not that the Jew's circumcision has been annulled in God's sight, but that he has become uncircumcised in heart (i.e. one whose heart is far from God and whose life is a contradiction of his membership of the Covenant people)'.

The meaning is not that the Gentile will assume the role of judge, but rather that he will be a witness for the prosecution in the sense that his obedience will be evidence of what the Jew ought to have been and could have been.[41]

Even commentators who deny that Christian Gentiles are specifically on view in 2:14–16 see a clear reference to the effect of the New Covenant on Gentiles in 2:25–29.[42] Once more the apostle asserts the importance of the inner life to God (2:28–29; cf. 2:15–16). In the argument that follows, circumcision of the heart corresponds to the work of the law written on the heart as an expression of transformation under the New Covenant. What counts with God is not being 'a Jew who is merely one outwardly', but being a Jew inwardly. True circumcision is not 'outward and physical', but 'a matter of the heart, by the Spirit, not by the letter'. Such a Jew looks for praise from God, not from other people. When God's righteous judgment is revealed, those who are circumcised in heart will be revealed and rewarded with eternal life (cf. 2:7).

Paul's argument is radical here, implying that physical circumcision is no longer necessary for receiving the benefits of the Abrahamic covenant (cf. Gen. 17:9–19). He does this because the call of the Old Testament itself is for the spiritual circumcision of the heart (Deut. 10:16; Jer. 4:4; 9:26), and Deuteronomy 30:6 declares that God will make this possible when he restores his people from the punishment of exile (cf. Ezek. 36:26–27; *Jubilees* 1.23). Since the spiritual reality towards which circumcision pointed has now been fulfilled in Christ, the blessings of the New Covenant are available for Jew and Gentile alike, without physical circumcision

---

41. Cranfield, *Romans*, vol. 1, p. 174.

42. E.g. Schreiner, *Romans*, pp. 140–145, argues that the letter–spirit antithesis in 2:27–29 does not refer to a particular way of interpreting Scripture, but shows the salvation-historical character of the text (cf. 7:6, 2 Cor. 3:6, both of which contrast the work of the Spirit with the Mosaic law). Cf. Dunn, *Romans 1–8*, pp. 122–125. Contrast Moo, *Romans*, pp. 169–175.

(cf. 3:30; 4:9–12; Gal. 5:2–6; 6:12–16; Phil. 3:3).[43] The gift of the Spirit circumcises the heart by making repentance, faith and obedience to God's revealed will possible (cf. 8:2–10).

God's love and God's Spirit in the heart

Romans 5:1–5 proclaims that those who are justified by faith have peace with God through our Lord Jesus Christ and 'rejoice in hope of the glory of God'. This hope is strengthened and confirmed through sufferings, and 'does not put those who cherish it to shame by proving illusory'.[44] The reason for this is that 'God's love has been poured into our hearts through the Holy Spirit who has been given to us.'

Although the verb 'poured out' is sometimes used with reference to the Spirit (Acts 2:17–18 [citing Joel 2:28–29]; 2:33; 10:45; Tit. 3:6), the subject here is explicitly 'God's love' and the Spirit is the agent ('through the Holy Spirit'). Since the apostle goes on to explain how God has shown his love for us *historically* in the death of his Son (5:6–11), Paul means that this objective demonstration of God's love is 'actually brought home to our hearts (so that we have recognised it and rejoice in it) by the Holy Spirit who has been given to us'.[45]

The Holy Spirit makes possible an experience of God's love that changes hearts and lives, sustaining hope in the midst of sufferings. From such experiences endurance and character are produced. Although most commentators rightly take 'the love of God' to refer to God's love for us, it is nevertheless true that 'God's gift of love

---

43. Compare the argument in Acts 10:10–15, 28, 15:8–11 about the cultic provisions of the Mosaic law being fulfilled in Christ, so that restrictions excluding Gentiles from the community of God's people no longer apply (cf. Eph. 2:11–22).

44. Cranfield, *Romans* vol. 1, pp. 261–262. Cranfield reads the verb 'put to shame' (*kataischynei*) as present tense, but it could be read as future, denoting the confidence believers can have at the judgment of God (cf. Schreiner, *Romans*, pp. 256–257).

45. Cranfield, *Romans*, vol. 1, p. 263. The passive implies that God the Father has poured out his love through the ministry of his Spirit.

kindles believers to love him in return.'[46] In this way, Deuteronomy 30:6 is fulfilled: God circumcises the heart of his people so that they can love him with all their heart and soul, and live to honour and praise him.

It is striking that the first reference to the love of God in Romans is 'in such vivid experiential terms'.[47] But this work of the Spirit clearly fulfils the promise of Ezekiel 11:19–20, 36:26–27 (cf. Joel 2:28–29), which is linked by Paul with Jeremiah 31:33 in 2 Corinthians 3.[48] What was implicit in Romans 2:14–15, 26–28, is made explicit here. Christ's sacrifice and the gift of the Holy Spirit have inaugurated the New Covenant for believing Jews and Gentiles. The Spirit is the 'first instalment' (2 Cor. 1:22; 5:5; Eph. 1:14, *arrabōn*) of the glory and the life to come in God's new creation.

Obedience from the heart

Romans 6 speaks about the transformation that is possible for those who are 'baptized into (Christ's) death'. They can 'walk in newness of life' (6:4) and no longer be 'enslaved to sin' (6:6). They can present themselves to God 'as those who have been brought from death to life' and offer every aspect of themselves 'as instruments for righteousness' (6:13). Now that they have been 'set free from sin and have become slaves of God', they produce the fruit of holiness and experience eternal life as its end (6:22).

When the apostle comes to describe how this change takes place *internally*, he gives thanks to God that 'you who were once slaves of sin have become obedient from the heart to the standard of teaching to which you were committed, and, having been set free from sin, have become slaves of righteousness' (6:17–18).

---

46. Schreiner, *Romans*, p. 257.
47. Dunn, *Romans 1–8*, p. 252.
48. D. Shaw, 'The New Covenant in Romans' (BA dissertation, Oak Hill College Library: London, 2011), p. 30, observes that Paul uses a conflation of New Covenant imagery in Rom. 5:5, as he does elsewhere. In this case it is 'the pouring out of the Spirit (Joel 2:28–30; Ezek. 39:29) to effect the renewal of the heart (Ezek. 36:26) and its reorientation toward God'.

'Obedient from the heart' sounds like a New Covenant expression. At the beginning of Romans, Paul declares that the purpose of his ministry is to bring about 'the obedience of faith for the sake of his [Christ's] name among all the nations' (1:5; cf. 16:26). The link between faith and obedience is then expressed in various ways throughout the letter. For example, gospel preaching is designed to elicit faith in the heart, enabling people to confess Christ as Lord and be saved (10:8–13). But the same passage goes on to describe the need for obedience to the gospel (10:16; cf. 15:18). The decision to believe the gospel is an act of obedience toward God. Indeed, 'true faith by its very nature includes in itself the sincere desire and will to obey God in all things'.[49]

'The standard of teaching' (ESV) would be better rendered 'the pattern of teaching' (NIV [2011], 'the pattern of teaching that has now claimed your allegiance'). The Greek expression *typon didachēs* is probably designed to convey the fact that the teaching they received moulded their lives in a particular way. It is clear from Romans 6 that the teaching in question concerns Christ's death and resurrection and the implications for believers. Paul is talking about commitment to Christ and the pattern of life established by the gospel, not commitment to some fixed catechetical formulation or creed (cf. Col. 2:6). The passive verb in the expression 'to which you were committed' (*paredothēte*) suggests the transfer of a slave from one master to another, in this case from 'sin' to 'righteousness'. Becoming a Christian means being placed under the authority of Christ through the gospel. Being obedient to this teaching is 'the outgrowth of God's action in "handing us over" to that teaching when we were converted'.[50]

---

49. Cranfield, *Romans*, vol. 1, p. 67. Moo, *Romans*, p. 52, takes the words 'obedience' and 'faith' to be mutually interpreting: 'obedience always involves faith, and faith always involves obedience'.

50. Moo, *Romans*, p. 401. Although Moo, pp. 401–402, thinks Paul may be contrasting the form of Christian teaching with the form of Jewish teaching, he agrees that *typos* may also have been used to suggest that Christian teaching 'moulds' and 'forms' those who have been handed over to it.

In the flow of the argument, Paul is concerned to stress the place of obedience in the Christian life. Note the imperatives in 6:12–13 and the revelation in 6:16 that you become 'slaves of the one whom you obey, either of sin, which leads to death, or of obedience, which leads to righteousness'. But in 6:17–18 Paul is grateful to God for the fact that *he* has already made 'obedience from the heart' possible by bringing the gospel to bear on the lives of those he addresses. By implication, the renewal of their hearts began when they were enabled to obey the gospel and began to be transformed by it. We may surmise that the Spirit's work in persuading us about the love of God (5:5) is critical to this response from the heart.[51]

Faith from the heart

In Romans 10:5 Paul cites two biblical texts to support his argument. The first is Leviticus 18:5 ('the person who does the commandments shall live by them'), which is said to describe 'the righteousness that is based on the law'. The second is Deuteronomy 30:11–14, which is said to describe 'the righteousness based on faith'. Much discussion has taken place about the way these two texts are used. Paul has a distinctive way of reading them in the light of Israel's failure and the fulfilment of God's covenant purpose in Christ (cf. 9:30 – 10:4). His approach is 'grounded in the narrative structure of Deuteronomy itself',[52] which predicts the judgment of exile because of Israel's unfaithfulness, but then promises divine restoration. Paul sees this restoration having taken place in Christ and explains Deuteronomy 30:11–14 in this light.

---

51. R. A. J. Gagnon, 'Heart of Wax and a Teaching that Stamps: Τυπος Διδαχης (Rom. 6:17b) Once More', *JBL* 112 (1993), pp. 667–687 (685–687), detects the New Covenant work of the Spirit here, in which the law is engraved on the heart. But he stops short of claiming a direct allusion to any one biblical passage. Schreiner, *Romans*, p. 334, rightly observes that 'God must be the one who causes obedience to rise in human hearts because all human beings are "slaves of sin".'

52. Schreiner, *Romans*, p. 557.

In the immediate context, as in Romans 2, attention is drawn to Gentile Christians, so as to challenge unbelieving Jews about their failure to obtain the blessings promised by God. 'Gentiles who did not pursue righteousness have attained it, that is, a righteousness that is by faith', whereas 'Israel who pursued a law that would lead to righteousness did not succeed in reaching that law' (9:30–31). The reason for that failure is 'because they did not pursue it by faith, but as if it were based on works' (9:32). Paul therefore proceeds to highlight 'the righteousness that comes from God', which is also described as 'the righteousness based on faith' (10:6).

Three times in the quotation and application of Deuteronomy 30:11–14 the word 'heart' is mention (10:8–10).[53] Paul is concerned to emphasize the need for belief from the heart, and confession with the mouth. The faith that justifies and saves is specifically a response to the gospel he proclaims, 'because, if you confess with your mouth that Jesus is Lord and believe in your heart that God raised him from the dead, you will be saved' (10:9). The need for such a response is reiterated when Paul says, 'For with the heart one believes and is justified, and with the mouth one confesses and is saved' (10:10).[54]

Those who persist in pursuing their own righteousness fail to see that in Christ the New Covenant has been inaugurated and fail to realize the implications. God has made possible through Christ the spiritual circumcision predicted by Moses (Deut. 30:6). He has placed the word of the gospel in hardened hearts and enabled people everywhere to believe and confess, to obey and to serve God. These riches are bestowed on Jews and Gentiles without distinction, thus

---

53. Additionally, the citation begins with the warning 'do not say in your heart' (Rom. 10:6), taken from Deut. 9:4, where Moses warns the Israelites not to boast about their own righteousness. The prospect of their heart turning away, so that they do not hear, but are 'drawn away to worship other gods and serve them' is also mentioned in Deut. 30:17.

54. Following the word order in Deut. 30:14, Paul in Rom. 10:9 puts confession with the mouth before belief. However, in the next verse he clarifies that belief in the heart must actually precede confession.

fulfilling the promise originally made to Abraham about the blessing of the nations (10:11–13).

There is a quotation from Joel 2:32 in Romans 10:13 ('everyone who calls on the name of the Lord will be saved'). In Joel's prophecy this comes immediately after the prediction about the eschatological pouring out of God's Spirit (Joel 2:28–29). Paul presumably viewed faith from the heart and calling upon Jesus as Lord as evidence of the Spirit's work in the life of those who responded to his gospel.

The renewal of the mind

The renewal of the mind in Romans 12:2 is bound up with the challenge to 'present your bodies as a living sacrifice, holy and acceptable to God, which is your spiritual worship' (12:1). This self-offering can be 'holy and acceptable' only because of the atoning work of Christ (3:23–26) and the sanctifying work of the Spirit (15:16).[55] In different terms, Paul repeats the challenge for believers to present themselves to God 'as those who have been brought from death to life' through the death and resurrection of Jesus (6:13). But if the service of our lives is to reflect our status as the holy people of God, we must heed this warning: 'Do not be conformed to this world, but be transformed by the renewal of your mind, that by testing you may discern what is the will of God, what is good and acceptable and perfect.'

Paul first warns against the danger of being 'conformed to this age' (*mē syschēmatizesthe tō aiōni toutō*). In effect, he recognizes 'the power of social groups, cultural norms, institutions, and traditions to mould the patterns of individual behavior'.[56] The passive 'do not be conformed' points to the effect these structures can have on believers: they can be squeezed into the world's mould in their

---

55. Cf. D. G. Peterson, *Possessed by God: A New Testament Theology of Sanctification and Holiness*, NSBT 1 (Leicester: Apollos; Downers Grove: InterVarsity Press, 1995), pp. 58–60.

56. J. D. G. Dunn, *Romans 9–16*, WBC 38B (Waco: Word, 1988), p. 712. Cf. Cranfield, *Romans*, vol. 2, pp. 605–608, on the two imperatives used in this verse.

thinking and behaviour. But the present imperative indicates that Christians can resist the world's values and behaviour patterns. Paul calls for a life in this world that is impelled and controlled by other factors.

God's transforming work is the powerful alternative to the influence of the world. Paul uses the same verb as he does in in 2 Corinthians 3:18 to describe this reshaping (*metamorphousthe*). Although the Holy Spirit is not named here, the renewal of the mind would seem to be critical to his work in believers (cf. Tit. 3:5). The Christian is to yield to the Spirit of God and his direction, rather than to the influence of this age and its norms (cf. Rom. 8:13–14). As we allow ourselves to be moulded by the norms and patterns of 'the age to come', we exhibit to the world the certainty and the character of the coming order that has already been manifested in Jesus Christ our Lord (cf. Col. 3:1–4).

Transformation of the life offered to God (12:1) takes place from within, by the renewal of the mind (12:2, *te anakainōsei tou noos*). As the following clause indicates, Paul is thinking about the mind as the faculty that enables us to test or 'prove what God's will is' (*dokimazein hymas ti to thelema tou theou*).[57] Elsewhere, the role Christians must play in reflecting on what pleases God is amplified (e.g. Phil. 4:8; Eph. 5:17). Renewal of the mind makes it possible for believers to go on discerning God's will and presenting themselves for daily obedience in the face of countless pressures to do otherwise.

Paul's challenge implies that the human mind, apart from such renewal, is unable to guide and keep us in the life that is pleasing to God. The language here echoes the charge that, since humanity 'did not see fit to acknowledge (*ouk edokimasan*) God, God gave them up to a debased mind (*eis adokimon noun*), to do what ought not to be done' (1:28). Despite their intellectual achievements, people live and act 'in the futility of their mind' (Eph. 4:17, *en mataioteti tou noos autōn*;

---

57. Dunn, *Romans 9–16*, p. 714, argues that the verb *dokimazein* (test, examine, approve) overlaps with the use of *diakrinein* (as used in 1 Cor. 14:29; cf. 1 Cor. 2:13–15; 12:10; *Didache* 11.7) to mean 'the capacity of forming the correct Christian ethical judgment at each given moment'.

cf. Col. 2:18; 1 Tim. 6:5; 2 Tim. 3:8; Tit. 1:15). But when they come
to know Jesus and are taught in accordance with the truth that is in
him, they can be renewed in the attitude or 'spirit' of their mind
(Eph. 4:23, *tō pneumati tou noos hymōn*).

So the first two verses of Romans 12 are closely linked and
together proclaim a reversal of the foolishness and rebellion depicted
in Romans 1:18–32.[58] Paul's ethic is not law determined, but its basis
is still 'the will of God'. If we seek to discover more closely what
the apostle meant by this, it is clear from what follows that 'Christians
find God's will in apostolic instruction, wisdom and in response to
the gospel'.[59]

God desires that believers should love and serve one another in
humility (12:3–13), respond in a Christlike way to persecutors (12:14–
21), give proper respect and pay dues to those in authority (13:1–7),
show neighbour love in every situation (13:8–10) and make 'no
provision for the flesh to gratify its desires', while being clothed with
the character of the Lord Jesus Christ (13:11–14; cf. Eph. 4:22–24;
Col. 3:5–17). Such apostolic teaching will be the means of discerning
God's will in a whole range of life situations.[60]

---

58. Cf. M. Thompson, *Clothed with Christ: The Example and Teaching of Jesus in Romans
    12:1 – 15:13*, JSNTSS 59 (Sheffield: Sheffield Academic Press, 1991), p. 82. It is
    also possible that 12:2 is meant to form a deliberate contrast with 2:18, where
    the Jews claim to know God's will and 'approve of what is superior' (*dokimazeis
    ta diapheronta*), because they are instructed in the law of God.

59. B. S. Rosner, 'Paul and the Law: What he Does Not Say', *JSNT* 32 (2010),
    pp. 405–419 (410). Rosner notes from Rom. 2:18–25 that Jews know God's
    will through the law and are under obligation to obey it as a written code.
    When Paul talks about Christians being enabled by the Spirit to 'fulfil' the
    law (Rom. 8:4; 13:8; Gal. 5:14; cf. Gal. 6:2), he treats the law as wisdom for
    living, rather than as 'that which must be done, kept and observed, and not
    transgressed' (Rosner, p. 418).

60. S. Kim, 'Paul's Common Paraenesis (1 Thess. 4 – 5; Phil. 2 – 4; and Rom.
    12 – 13): The Correspondence Between Romans 1:18–32 and 12:1–2, and
    the Unity of Romans 12–13', *TynB* 62.1 (2011), pp. 109–139, shows that
    Paul had a set of moral exhortations for all the churches, as suggested by
    1 Cor. 4:17, though he adapted these to suit the situation of the different
    churches he addressed.

Conclusion

Romans 1 – 2 first establishes why Jews and Gentiles need radical 'heart surgery', before identifying the way in which God has met that need through the fulfilment of various New Covenant promises. Atonement through the sacrifice of Christ is fundamental to the argument in Romans 3 – 8. Jesus' death provides justification by faith, forgiveness, redemption from sin's penalty and dominion, and release from condemnation to serve God in the new life made possible by the Spirit. In effect, Paul shows how the fulfilment of God's promise to 'forgive their iniquity' and 'remember their sin no more' (Jer. 31:34) is the basis of every blessing received in Christ.

The way God works in human hearts is variously explained. Specifically recalling the promise of Jeremiah 31:33, Paul talks about 'the work of the law', which is 'written on the heart' of believers (2:15). Later passages reveal that this change involves the whole-hearted devotion of minds and bodies to God and to the doing of his will (6:12–18; 12:1–2). As in 2 Corinthians 3, Paul is not simply thinking about a new ability to keep the law of Moses, but a new way of serving and pleasing God, empowered and directed by his Spirit (7:6; 8:4–14). Spiritual circumcision is a parallel concept in Romans 2:29, where the promise of Deuteronomy 30:6 is recalled, and the possibility of loving God 'with all your heart and with all your soul' is implied.

Romans 5:5 mentions the Holy Spirit as the one through whom the love of God has been poured into the hearts of believers. This work of the Spirit sustains hope in the midst of sufferings, and from such experiences endurance and character are produced. Paul possibly conflates several texts to make his point (Ezek. 11:19–20; 36:26–27; 39:29; cf. Joel 2:28–29).

Romans 6:17 draws attention to the 'pattern of teaching' that has claimed the allegiance of Christians. This is said to produce obedience from the heart. In the preceding verses Paul's focus is on the way believers are to live in the light of their baptism into Christ's death. This suggests that the gospel about Christ crucified and resurrected is the teaching that forms or moulds Christian character and behaviour. Although there is no specific allusion to a New Covenant passage here, the image of the law engraved on the heart could have influenced the way Paul portrays the transforming effect of the gospel on the heart.

Romans 10 employs a number of biblical texts in a salvation-historical argument, to proclaim the fulfilment of God's covenant purpose for Jews and Gentiles in Christ. Here the challenge is to believe with the heart and confess with the mouth that Jesus is Lord. Paul's use of Joel 2:32 in this context suggests that he may have been thinking about the Spirit making it possible for people to call upon Jesus for salvation in this way.

A promise about God banishing ungodliness from Jacob when he takes away their sins is another expression of the New Covenant in Romans 11:26–27 (citing Isa. 59:20–21, with a portion of 27:9). At this climactic point in the argument, God's faithfulness to Israel is affirmed by conflating a different set of prophetic texts.

Paul's teaching about the impact of sin on the human heart in Romans is also expressed in terms of minds becoming debased and unable to lead people to behave rightly (1:21–25, 28). Nevertheless, those who yield themselves to Christ can have their minds renewed and come to discern 'what is the will of God, what is good and acceptable and perfect' (12:2).

Paul uses another type of New Covenant argument in Galatians 4:21–31 to convince Gentile Christians that they should hold fast to the freedom they have in Christ. Those who are 'born according to the Spirit' are beneficiaries of the covenant made with the 'children of promise', who belong to 'the Jerusalem above' (cf. Heb. 12:22–24). They should not submit to a demand for law-keeping (Gal. 5:1–15), but 'walk by the Spirit' (5:16–26).

So Paul uses New Covenant texts and allusions polemically, but also to encourage Christians about the work of God taking place in their hearts and minds. This transforming work derives from the death and resurrection of Jesus and the gift of God's Spirit. Spiritual circumcision is a sign of New Covenant membership. The Spirit uses the gospel to convert and mould believers in the way of Christ. There is therefore an inward and an outward effect that assures believers of God's intention to sustain, and yet continually change, them, until they are finally 'conformed to the image of his Son' (8:29).[61]

Pastorally, therefore, we are encouraged to see how the gospel, applied by the Holy Spirit to human hearts, is used by God to transform the disposition and behaviour of his people and assure them of his grace towards them. As we learn to conform our lives to the message about Christ's death and resurrection, God works to renew hearts and minds by his Spirit. This is a reminder of the need for New Covenant ministry to focus on teaching and applying the gospel to Christians, as well as proclaiming it to unbelievers.

Paul's teaching in Romans confirms the observation made in connection with 2 Corinthians 3:18, that it is through the gospel that we continue to 'gaze' at Christ and are transformed into his likeness. The New Testament writers continually draw out the implications of the gospel in dealing with pastoral problems, sometimes by specifically alluding to the fulfilment of New Covenant promises and highlighting the implications for believers. This pattern of ministry provides a model for effective teaching, counselling and spiritual nurture in our churches today.

But the promises of the New Covenant are not simply recalled by Paul to encourage personal growth or congregational maturation in Christ. They are used to guarantee God's commitment to fulfil his saving plan for Israel and the nations. Gospel ministry is to continue with the assurance that the blessings of the New Covenant can be enjoyed in the present by people from every nation, and that God will ultimately bring the full number of those chosen in Christ to benefit from those blessings in a renewed creation.

---

61. Cf. Peterson, *Possessed by God*, pp. 109–120.

6. THE TRANSFORMING KNOWLEDGE OF GOD

There is an important allusion to Jeremiah's prophecy in the first letter of John, where the writer claims that his readers have been anointed by the Holy One and 'all have knowledge' (2:20). The context has much to say about this knowledge, leading to the climactic claim that

> the anointing that you received from him abides in you, and you have no need that anyone should teach you. But as his anointing teaches you about everything, and is true, and is no lie – just as it has taught you, abide in him. (2:27)

Examining these and related claims in John's letter, I will argue that Jeremiah's prediction of a new covenant had a considerable influence on the writer's way of thinking about the Christian life. Turning to the Fourth Gospel, I will explore ways in which some of the same themes are developed there.

My presumption in examining the Gospel of John and the first letter of John together is that they were both written by the same person. According to the earliest witnesses, the author of both documents was John the apostle, the son of Zebedee, who designated himself 'the disciple whom Jesus loved' (John 13:23; 21:20). Although this evidence is rejected by many contemporary scholars, the hypothesis that the Gospel was written by the apostle John 'has never been decisively refuted and continues to be at least as plausible as the alternative explanations'.[1] Striking similarities of language and concepts in the first letter, and the author's claim to be one of the original witnesses of Christ (1 John 1:1–4), support the tradition about apostolic authorship of that document as well.[2]

Knowledge of the truth about Jesus

False alternatives

When John refers to the anointing that brings knowledge of the truth, it is in the context of warning about deceptive false teachers (1 John 2:18–27) or 'false prophets' (4:1). John's readers have heard about the antichrist, who will come at the end of the age to oppose God and his people (2:18; cf. 2 Thess. 2:3–10; Rev. 13:1–18), but now John informs them about 'many antichrists', who have come in anticipation of that final enemy.[3] The false teachers are identified

---

1. A. J. Köstenberger, *John*, BECNT (Grand Rapids: Baker Academic, 2004), p. 7. Cf. D. A. Carson, *The Gospel According to John*, PNTC (Grand Rapids: Eerdmans; Leicester: Inter-Varsity Press, 1991), pp. 68–81. Carson, pp. 665–685, even argues against the view that the Gospel was put into its final form by someone else.

2. Cf. C. G. Kruse, *The Letters of John*, PNTC (Grand Rapids: Eerdmans; Leicester: Apollos, 2000), pp. 9–14.

3. Kruse, ibid., pp. 99–102, helpfully compares what Jesus teaches in Matt. 24 and Mark 13 with passages elsewhere in the NT that reflect the expectation of a powerful end-time figure opposed to God and his people. But only 1 and 2 John actually use the term 'antichrist'.

as 'antichrists' and are further described as those who were once members of John's Christian community, but who have now seceded from it (2:19).

These 'antichrists' denied that Jesus is the Christ (2:22a), but this involved more than disputing his messiahship. They denied the Father and the Son by refusing to confess Jesus as the Son of God (2:22b–23). In view of later arguments, it appears that they disputed the reality of the incarnation (4:2–3) by rejecting the multifaceted testimony of God concerning his Son (5:6–10). They may also have denied that the Son shed his blood as an atoning sacrifice for sin (4:10; 5:6–8; cf. 1:7; 2:2). Perhaps they still considered themselves to be Christian, but the apostle calls them liars (2:22) and deceivers (2:26). As those who did not 'have the Son of God', they did not have the eternal life God made available in his Son (5:11–12).[4]

The anointing of the Spirit

John does not write because his readers are ignorant of the truth, but because he is convinced they know it, and 'because no lie is of the truth' (2:21). The reason he can be so sure they know the truth is that they literally 'have an anointing from the Holy One' (2:20). The word 'anointing' (*chrisma*) is only found here and in 2:27, but elsewhere in the New Testament the corresponding verb (*chriō*, 'anoint') is used in connection with the work of the Holy Spirit (Luke 4:18; Acts 10:38; 2 Cor. 1:21–22). Although it has been argued that the anointing refers to God's word, 'as it is received by faith into men's hearts and remains active, *thanks to the work of the Spirit*',[5] it is more likely that John simply refers to the Holy Spirit, 'given to

---

4. Various hypotheses about these opponents and their teaching are discussed by Kruse, ibid., pp. 15–27.

5. I. de la Potterie, 'Anointing of the Christian by Faith', in I. de la Potterie and S. Lyonnet, *The Christian Lives by the Spirit* (New York: Alba House, 1971), pp. 114–115 (emphasis original). I. H. Marshall, *The Epistles of John*, NICNT (Grand Rapids: Eerdmans, 1978), pp. 154–155, endorses the argument of de la Potterie.

believers when they first believed and who continues to teach them what they need to know'.[6]

In the Gospel of John Jesus promises his disciples that the Holy Spirit will teach them all things (14:26), testify about him (15:26–27) and guide them 'into all the truth' (16:13–15). These promises seem to be specifically related to their role as authorized witnesses and interpreters of Christ after his ascension. But the promise in 1 John 2:20, 27 refers to an ongoing work of the Spirit in all believers, confirming the truth of the gospel preached to them and warning them of aberrations that distort the apostolic message. The anointing mentioned here is not a special gifting or enabling of prophets or preachers, but the regular work of the Spirit in every beneficiary of the New Covenant. The teaching of the Fourth Gospel about the Spirit is taken up in 1 John and applied to the specific situation of believers encountering false teaching.[7]

John's letter avoids the danger of subjectivism in this regard by stressing the foundational nature of the *apostolic testimony to Jesus* (1:1–5; 2:24–25; 3:11; 4:5–6, 14–16; 5:6–12). When he says 'the word of God abides in you' (2:14), we may conclude this happens because the Spirit writes the message of the gospel on human hearts. But John is clear about the stages by which this conviction comes: those who have the Spirit of God listen to the apostolic testimony and believe it, confessing that Jesus Christ has come in the flesh (4:16). In essence, therefore, the knowledge that John has in mind is a certainty about the character and will of God, as proclaimed in the apostolic gospel.

Following a widely attested range of ancient manuscripts, the AV reads, 'and ye know all things' (2:20; cf. ASV, NKJV). But most modern

---

6. Kruse, *Letters of John*, p. 110, concluding a lengthy evaluation of the argument of de la Potterie. Knowledge is also traced back to the Spirit in 3:24; 4:13.

7. Cf. J. C. Coetzee, 'The Holy Spirit in 1 John', *Neot* 13 (1979), pp. 53–55; Kruse, *Letters of John*, pp. 152–155. Even if the Gospel was written after the epistle, the teaching about the Spirit found in the Gospel must surely have been known in the community addressed by the epistle.

English versions follow the alternative found in a smaller number of particularly reliable ancient manuscripts (NIV, 'and all of you know [the truth]'; NRSV, ESV, 'you all have knowledge'). The latter is more likely to have been the original because John is speaking about a particular knowledge concerning the Son and the Father, not a knowledge of 'all things'. Moreover, he is contrasting the certainty given to all believers by the Holy Spirit with the esoteric knowledge claimed by those who have left the apostolic fellowship.[8]

Here then is the first echo of Jeremiah's expectation that 'they shall all know me, from the least of them to the greatest' (Jer. 31:34). The prophet predicts that all of God's people under the New Covenant will have the same transforming knowledge of the Lord. John understands the fulfilment in terms of the anointing with God's Spirit at conversion and the ongoing preservation of believers from false teaching about the person and work of Christ. Like Paul in 2 Corinthians 3, John appears to draw on the predictions of Ezekiel 11:19–20, 36:26–27 to explain how Jeremiah's promise has been fulfilled.

Hearing and remaining

The primacy of the apostolic testimony is stressed when John urges, 'Let what you heard from the beginning abide in you,' and promises, 'If what you heard from the beginning abides in you, then you too will abide in the Son and in the Father' (2:24). The outcome of such 'abiding' is eternal life, just as God promised (2:25; cf. 1:2; 2:28; 4:15–16; 5:11–13, 20). If the message heard by John's readers when they first believed in Christ continues to control and direct their relationship with God, they are assured of remaining in that

---

8. Kruse, *Letters of John*, pp. 103–104, argues for 'all things' (*panta*) by observing a possible parallel with 2:27. But Marshall, *Epistles of John*, p. 156, n. 26, considers a more immediate parallel use of 'all' (*pantes*) in 2:19 and argues that the stress in 2:20 is on 'the fact of knowing rather than on the object of knowledge'. Copyists may have inserted *panta* because the verb had no object. Cf. B. M. Metzger (ed.), *A Textual Commentary on the Greek New Testament*, 2nd ed. (Stuttgart: Deutsche Bibelgesellschaft, 1994), p. 641.

relationship. As in the Fourth Gospel, eternal life is a present possibility for those who believe in the Son, but its ultimate outcome is 'the resurrection of life' (John 5:24–29).[9]

John reminds his readers that he writes these things about those who are trying to deceive them (2:26). The false teaching they are encountering could potentially lead some away from a saving relationship with God. The issue is as serious as that! Nevertheless, he amplifies his previous encouragement to them when he says, 'But the anointing that you received from him abides in you, and you have no need that anyone should teach you' (2:27). By his Spirit, God continues to dwell in them (3:24b), and this is 'their fundamental defence against deception'.[10]

When he claims that they have no need that anyone should teach them, he is once more echoing the promise of Jeremiah 31:34, 'And no longer shall each one teach his neighbour and each his brother, saying, "Know the LORD," for they shall all know me, from the least of them to the greatest, declares the LORD.' John does not even see the need to teach them the truth *himself* (2:21), since they received it when they were converted. He simply encourages them to let what they heard from the beginning remain in them (2:24). At the same time, he warns them not to listen to deceptive reinterpretations of the gospel by false teachers.

Along with the exhortation to let the gospel control and direct their thinking and behaviour, John assures them that the Spirit's anointing 'teaches you about everything' (2:27). In the immediate context, this will mean everything they need to know about the Son and the Father to have eternal life. In the rest of John's letter this knowledge seems also to include the need for righteous and loving behaviour, issuing from a genuine relationship with the Father through the Son. Most importantly, John insists that what the anointing by the Spirit teaches them is true and not a lie: the Spirit's

---

9. Cf. C. H. Dodd, *The Interpretation of the Fourth Gospel* (Cambridge: Cambridge University Press, 1963), pp. 144–150; Kruse, *Letters of John*, pp. 184–187.

10. Kruse, *Letters of John*, p. 108.

role is to confirm and apply the message of the gospel to the hearts of believers so that they remain in Christ and are not led astray.

Teaching under the New Covenant

Word and Spirit belong together in John's view of Christian conversion and perseverance. Rather than bringing some new teaching to challenge them, John exhorts his readers to remain in Christ (2:27), by letting what they heard from the beginning remain in them (2:24).

However, considering that John himself is engaged in a form of teaching when he writes this letter, is he being consistent when he says, 'you have no need that anyone should teach you'? Is he de-emphasizing the role of authoritative teachers as 'an instrusive novelty on the Johannine scene'?[11] Is he indicating that there are two forms of instruction that must go together: ongoing instruction by Christian teachers accompanied by the inner instruction of the Holy Spirit?[12] Is he speaking about teaching in a narrowly defined way?

Returning to the context of Jeremiah's prophecy, Carson argues that those who will no longer be needed under the New Covenant are not simply teachers, but 'intermediary teachers', such as the prophets and priests of Israel were.[13] The secessionists who were troubling John's readers were claiming a special knowledge that only

---

11. R. E. Brown, *The Epistles of John*, AB 30 (New York: Doubleday, 1982), pp. 509–510. Brown, pp. 374–376, argues that the lack of authoritative teachers in John's community was what made the propaganda of the secessionists such a threat. He concludes that the author's vision of a Christianity without authorized teachers ultimately failed.

12. This view goes back to Augustine of Hippo (*In Epistolam* 3.13; SC 75, p. 210).

13. D. A. Carson, 'You Have No Need That Anyone Should Teach You' (1 John 2:27): An Old Testament Allusion That Determines the Interpretation', in P. J. Williams, A. D. Clarke, P. M. Head and D. Instone-Brewer (eds.), *The New Testament in Its First Century Setting: Essays on Context and Background in Honour of B. W. Winter on His 65th Birthday* (Grand Rapids: Eerdmans, 2004), pp. 269–280 (279).

they could impart. They were elevating themselves to the role of mediating teacher,

> to the position of those who do more than expound the truth that is in the domain of the entire church and accessible to the entire church: they claim to teach from the vantage point of superiors, the elite of the elect, the mediators. And that class of teacher, the sixth-century prophets foresaw, would forever be abolished.[14]

Carson's point is well made with reference to claims of new knowledge or superior insight into the meaning of the Christian revelation. The role that is given to the Spirit in 1 John 2 is 'primarily as a testimony to the tradition, not as a source of new revelation'.[15] But more can be said.

Apostles and prophets functioned as mediating teachers in giving an authentic, Spirit-directed witness to Christ in the first place. Their testimony, which in due course was recorded in what we call the New Testament, became the touchstone of orthodoxy (1 John 4:1–6) and the foundation of the Spirit-indwelt community of Christ's people (Eph. 2:21–22). Teaching and exhortation on the basis of this God-given revelation is not mediatorial in the sense outlined by Carson, but is vital for the maturation of the body of Christ and for the preservation of his people from error (Eph. 4:11–16).

Unlike the Pauline letters or Hebrews, the Johannine letters do not explicitly encourage the recipients to work out the implications of their relationship with God by teaching and exhorting one another. Issues of leadership and authority emerge in the three letters, and both the second and third give evidence of travelling missionaries and teachers. John does not oppose the fact that others are engaged in such ministries, but particularly in the first and second letters is concerned about preserving the foundational 'teaching of Christ' (2 John 9) from being corrupted or left behind.

---

14. Ibid., p. 280.
15. Kruse, *Letters of John*, p. 112.

Realizing all the benefits of the New Covenant

Although the word 'covenant' does not appear in 1 John, certain covenantal patterns of thought certainly do.[16] First, there is the mention of special revelation conveyed to a distinct group of people, to enable them to be in a relationship with God that issues in obedience to his commandments (1:1 – 2:14). Secondly, the community of the faithful is encouraged to be different from the world and from those who have seceded from their fellowship (2:15–27). Thirdly, God's people are identified as those who practise righteousness and show love for one another (2:28 – 3:24). Fourthly, those who truly belong to God listen to his voice, know God as he has revealed himself, love God and fellow believers, and persevere in that relationship by his gracious enabling (4:1 – 5:21).

At one level it could be argued that the whole of 1 John applies certain covenantal themes found in Exodus and Deuteronomy to the Christian fellowship. More precisely, it can be argued that John presents these themes in terms of their New Covenant fulfilment. Since John was influenced by Jeremiah's prophecy in opposing the teaching of the 'antichrists', it is likely that each of the New Covenant promises has had its impact on the way he writes.

The atoning sacrifice

Under the Mosaic covenant the problem of sin was dealt with by the prescribed pattern of sacrifices, culminating in the ritual of the annual Day of Atonement (Leviticus 1 – 7, 16).[17] John confronts the problem of sin in the community he addresses by referring to 'the blood of Jesus (God's) Son', which 'cleanses us from all sin' (1:7). The 'blood of Jesus', which refers to his death on the cross, provides 'purification from sins for those who walk

---

16. Cf. H. A. A. Kennedy, 'The Covenant-Conception in the First Epistle of John', *ExpT* 28 (1916), pp. 23–26.

17. Cf. D. G. Peterson, *Engaging with God: A Biblical Theology of Worship* (Leicester: Apollos; Downers Grove: InterVarsity Press, 1992), pp. 36–42.

in the light with God'.[18] Using the present tense, John represents both walking and cleansing as ongoing and related activities: those who walk in the light do not hide their sin from God, but continually avail themselves of the benefits of Christ's atoning sacrifice (cf. 2:2).

Closest to Jeremiah's promise that God will 'forgive their iniquity' and 'remember their sin no more' is John's assurance to those who confess their sins: 'he [God] is faithful and just to forgive us our sins and to cleanse us from all unrighteousness' (1:9). Indeed, in Jeremiah 33:8 (LXX 40:8) there is an even more exact parallel: 'I will cleanse them from all the guilt of their sin against me, and I will forgive all the guilt of their sin and rebellion against me.' God's forgiveness involves no longer holding sin against those who are in Christ, while his cleansing from all unrighteousness means removing the defilement that sin produces. Thus every impediment to fellowship with God is removed.

God's *faithfulness* in forgiving sin and cleansing from all unrighteousness has a covenantal reference. Most obviously it alludes to the promises found in Jeremiah and the other eschatological prophets. But behind them all lies the foundational promise made to Moses when the covenant with Israel was being renewed:

> The LORD, the LORD, a God merciful and gracious, slow to anger,
> and abounding in steadfast love and faithfulness, keeping steadfast
> love for thousands, forgiving iniquity and transgression and sin.
> (Exod. 34:6–7)

God is also said to be '*just* to forgive us our sins and to cleanse us from all unrighteousness'. It might be thought that the justice of God would mean visiting the consequences of sin upon sinners, as Exodus 34:7 goes on to suggest. However, using the same Greek

---

18. Kruse, *Letters of John*, p. 64. Kruse notes the various uses of the verb 'cleanse' (*katharizō*) in the NT and concludes that in one way or another the term is used to describe 'purification which makes people or things acceptable in God's sight'.

word (*dikaios*), John goes on to describe 'Jesus Christ *the righteous*' as 'an advocate with the Father' (2:1). God acts righteously in forgiving sin by providing Christ as both our advocate and as 'the propitiation for our sins' (2:2).

The word translated 'advocate' is the Greek term *paraklētos*, which is used four times in the Gospel of John to refer to the promised Holy Spirit (John 14:16, 26; 15:26; 16:7).[19] Only here in the New Testament is it used to refer to the ascended Christ, though John 14:16 refers to the Spirit as 'another Helper', implying that Jesus was the helper or advocate of the disciples in the course of his earthly ministry. 'Intercessor' might be an appropriate rendering here (cf. Exod. 32:30–32, Job 42:7–10, and the use of different terminology in Rom. 8:34; Heb. 7:25). The living Lord Jesus is the one who 'now stands in the presence of the Father to speak on behalf of those who have not acted righteously'.[20] But John also makes it clear that his continuing advocacy is possible because he is himself 'the propitiation for our sins' (2:2, *hilasmos peri tōn hamartiōn hēmōn*; cf. 4:10).

The NRSV and NIV render this expression 'the atoning sacrifice for our sins'. In the LXX the term *hilasmos* is used for the removal of guilt because of sin (cf. Lev. 25:9; Num. 5:8; Ps. 129:4 [ET 130:4]; Ezek. 44:27; Amos 8:14; 2 Maccabees 3.33). However, the idea of placating the wrath of God is often present when this word group is used in the Bible. So the ESV follows the AV in rendering the term 'the propitiation for our sins'. This suggests that Christ's death both turns away God's anger and secures forgiveness and cleansing. In 4:10 God takes the initiative in showing his love for us and sending his Son to deal with the problem of sin through his sacrificial death. In 2:2 Christ's sacrifice is juxtaposed with his heavenly advocacy, suggesting that Jesus secures mercy for sinners by his death and

---

19. K. Grayston, 'The Meaning of *Paraklētos*', *JSNT* 13 (1981), pp. 67–82, has surveyed the use of the term *paraklētos* in early Greek writings and concluded that it was a word of general meaning that could appear in legal contexts with the specific meaning of 'supporter or sponsor'.

20. Kruse, *Letters of John*, p. 73.

continues to plead the benefits of his sacrifice before the Father in heaven.[21]

Linking together what is said in 1 John 1:7, 9 and 2:1–2, the argument is that the 'blood' of Jesus retains its redeeming and cleansing power because he is alive and remains 'with the Father' (2:1), always available to apply the benefit of his once-for-all sacrifice to those who walk in the light and confess their sins to him (cf. Heb. 4:14–16; 7:25). In Jeremiah 31:34 God promises, 'I will forgive their iniquity (*hileōs esomai tais adikiais autōn*), and I will remember their sin no more.' In 1 John 2:2 John uses a related term to describe the character of the sacrifice that makes such forgiveness possible for those who trust in Christ.[22]

The renewed heart

John highlights the knowledge that delivers from sin and brings eternal life. This knowledge comes from hearing the apostolic testimony and being anointed by the Spirit of God. But it is more than a knowledge of certain facts about God. A relationship with the Father through the Son is implied by concepts such as fellowship with the Father and the Son (1:3), remaining in the Son and in the

---

21. J. R. Michaels, 'Atonement in John's Gospel and Epistles', in C. E. Hill and F. A. James (eds.), *The Glory of the Atonement: Biblical, Theological and Practical Perspectives* (Leicester: Apollos; Downers Grove: InterVarsity Press, 2004), pp. 106–118 (114), makes the point that 2:1 'makes God the *object*, not the subject of the reconciliation taking place, and to that extent supports "propitiation" as the means of *hilasmos*' (original emphasis). Kruse, *Letters of John*, pp. 75–76, compares the use of cognate terms in the LXX and concludes that atonement in the OT includes 'both the cleansing and forgiveness of the sinner, and the turning away of God's anger'. Cf. H.-G. Link, *NIDNTT* 3:149; Marshall, *Epistles of John*, pp. 117–119.

22. Although 2:2 goes on to say, 'and not for ours only but also for the sins of the whole world', 5:11–13 makes it clear that only those who 'have' the Son and believe in his 'name' have eternal life. Presumably, John means that Christ's sacrifice was sufficient to deal with the sins of the whole world, but its benefit is experienced only when people come to faith in Christ.

Father (2:24), knowing God (4:7–8), loving God (4:19 – 5:2), and 'having' the Father and the Son (2:23; 5:12).[23]

Both Jeremiah and Ezekiel predicted that God would act radically to deal with the problem of sin, to bring a new knowledge of God and to change the heart of his people. The knowledge of God that John proclaims includes a certainty about God's love expressed in the provision of forgiveness and cleansing through the death of his Son. Such knowledge makes it possible for Christians to continue walking 'in the light', to remain in him and to keep his commandments, especially the command to love (2:1–12). Knowing the love of God in sending his Son to deal with the problem of sin is a motivation and empowerment for godly living (3:11–18; 4:7–12).

The interiority of the New Covenant is expressed in many ways by John.[24] For example, God's word is not in those who deny that they have sinned (1:10), but his word remains in those who truly know God, and who have 'overcome the evil one' (2:14). The inward effect of the gospel is also described negatively in terms of 'the truth' not being in someone (1:8; 2:4; contrast 2 John 2). But when someone 'keeps' God's word, 'in him truly the love of God is perfected' (2:5). The love of the Father is not in some people (2:15; 3:17), but when God abides in us, 'his love is perfected in us' (4:12). Those who hate and murder do not have eternal life abiding in them (3:15), but 'whoever abides in love abides in God, and God abides in him' (4:16). Put another way, God abides in Christians 'by the Spirit whom he has given us' (3:24; cf. 4:4, 13).

In several contexts John talks about those who are 'born of God': they practise righteousness (2:29), cannot keep on sinning (3:9; 5:18), know that 'God is love' and love others accordingly (4:7–8), believe

---

23. Cf. M.-E. Boismard, 'La connaissance de Dieu dans l'Alliance Nouvelle d'après la première épître de S. Jean', *RevB* 56 (1949), pp. 365–391; '"Je ferai avec vous une alliance nouvelle" (introduction à la première épître de S. Jean)', *LumVie* 8 (1953), pp. 94–109.

24. E. Malatesta, *Interiority and Covenant: A Study of εἶναι ἐν and μένειν ἐν in the First Letter of Saint John*, AnBib 69 (Rome: Pontifical Biblical Institute, 1978), investigates the use of relevant terminology extensively.

that Jesus is the Christ (5:1) and overcome the world by the exercise of faith (5:4). Seeking to distinguish those who are born of God from those who are not, John speaks of the 'seed' of God that remains in believers and keeps them from sinning (3:9). This appears to be a metaphor for 'the Holy Spirit who effects spiritual birth in those who believe'.[25] There is a parallel here with the teaching about being 'born of the Spirit' in John 3:3–8.

Finally, it should be noted that John talks explicitly about the impact of the gospel on the 'heart' of believers in 3:19–22. As part of the exhortation to love one another in 3:11–24, John asks how God's love can be present in someone who sees a fellow believer in need and has no pity or compassion (v. 17).[26] Christians are to love in deed and truth, not simply in word or talk (v. 18). Indeed, we will know that we belong to the truth when our love finds practical expression in helping someone in need (v. 19).

When we act in love, we will literally 'persuade our heart' (*peisomen tēn kardian hēmōn*) before God. This claim is made because John envisages that our heart might condemn us for falling short of God's loving standard.[27] Even though our loving actions may be inadequate and weak, we need to remember that 'God is greater than our heart, and he knows everything' (v. 20). Hearts may be reassured before him by acting in love, while trusting in his perfect knowledge

---

25. Kruse, *Letters of John*, p. 154. Kruse, pp. 112–132, rightly argues that 1 John 2:28 – 3:10 is about the Spirit's role in bringing spiritual children to birth and rendering them incapable of apostasy. Marshall, *Epistles of John*, pp. 186–187, identifies the seed as the Spirit who is 'operative in the preaching of the Word which produces the new birth in the hearts of those who hear it and respond with faith (1 Thess. 1:5f.)'.

26. ESV 'closes his heart against him' is not as helpful a rendering of the Greek (*kleisē ta splanchna autou ap' autou*) as NIV 'has no pity on him'. The affections rather than the thoughts and intentions of the heart are in view here.

27. Kruse, *Letters of John*, p. 139, denies that heart can be a synonym for conscience here, but there is an important parallel in Heb. 10:22 ('hearts sprinkled clean from an evil conscience'). Cf. C. Maurer, *TDNT* 7:908–919. So Kruse, p. 141, somewhat strangely interprets the condemning heart as objecting to legitimate calls upon its generosity.

of us and his boundless mercy. Thus reassured, we may have confidence before God, both now in prayer and ultimately on the day of judgment (*parrēsia*, as in 2:28; 3:21; 4:17; 5:14; cf. Heb. 3:6; 4:16; 10:19, 35).

The New Covenant in 1 John

1 John alludes to every aspect of Jeremiah's prophecy about the New Covenant and reflects the logic of that oracle. Ezekiel's predictions about the Spirit's role in the renewal of God's people are drawn in to help explain the fulfilment. There is explicit mention of Jeremiah's promise that all of God's people will know him and will not need teachers to mediate new revelation to them. The source of this knowledge is identified as the apostolic testimony to Jesus and his saving work, confirmed and applied by the Spirit, whom each believer receives. Fundamental to that transforming knowledge is the love of God demonstrated towards us in the sacrificial death of Jesus and his ongoing role as advocate with the Father. The Spirit effects regeneration and causes the truth of the gospel and its many benefits to be implanted in the heart. Believers are moved by word and Spirit to avoid error and disobedience, to live righteously and to practise love. This anticipates the complete transformation into his likeness that is to come, when Christ returns (3:1–3).

The incarnation of the Word

As in the letters of John, the word 'covenant' does not appear in the Fourth Gospel, but many of the major themes of the Gospel are covenantal.[28] Some appear immediately in the prologue, where there is an obvious contrast between the giving of the law through Moses and the coming of grace and truth through the incarnation of the Son of God. Throughout the Gospel there are many hints

---

28. Cf. J. W. Pryor, *John: Evangelist of the Covenant People* (London: Darton, Longman and Todd, 1992).

that the renewal predicted by Jeremiah and Ezekiel has been made possible by the work of Christ and the gift of God's Spirit.

The Word and the light

John's Gospel begins with a remarkable reflection on the role and significance of the eternal Word, 'made flesh' in the person of Jesus Christ. A number of religious contexts have been suggested as the background for understanding the use of this term, but several factors point to Scripture as the primary influence.[29] The prologue reminds us of Old Testament teaching about God's creative, revelatory and redemptive word, which is the means of his self-expression and relationship with the world (e.g. Gen. 1:1–31; Ps. 33:4–22; Isa. 55:6–13).

The person identified as 'the Word' was 'in the beginning' with God, but also shared the essence of God (1:1–2): 'the Word was with God and the Word was God'.[30] The Word is the one through whom God created all things (1:3). Moreover, 'In him was life, and the life was the light of men' (1:4; cf. 5:26). Although some have taken this as a reference to natural or general revelation, the light motif in the Old Testament regularly expresses the idea of special revelation and is linked with life and salvation (e.g. Pss 27:1; 36:9; Isa. 49:6).[31]

---

29. Cf. Carson, *John*, pp. 114–116; Köstenberger, *John*, pp. 26–27. Carson, p. 116, makes the point that 'the word' was one of many terms with a broad semantic range that the early Christians could shape '*by their own usage* to make it convey, *in the context of their own work*, what they knew to be true of Jesus Christ' (original emphasis).

30. R. E. Brown, *The Gospel According to John*, AB 29A (New York: Doubleday, 1966), pp. 4–5, notes that the preposition in the expression *pros ton theon* (with God) establishes a relationship between God and the Word, while distinguishing the two from each other. The verb *ēn* (was) then conveys the notions of existence and predication. D. B. Wallace, *Greek Grammar Beyond the Basics* (Grand Rapids: Zondervan, 1996), p. 269, argues that the noun *theos* (God) without the article indicates that Jesus 'shared the *essence* of the Father, though they differed in person'.

31. Köstenberger, *John*, pp. 30–32, acknowledges that 'light' and 'life' are universal religious terms, but argues that John's teaching is deeply rooted in OT teaching about these notions.

The need for rescue from darkness is stressed by the words that follow: 'The light shines in the darkness, and the darkness has not overcome it' (1:4). This anticipates the theme of conflict and victory in the ensuing story of Jesus. The Word brings life and light in the context of a cosmic conflict, but the expectation is that the light will triumph. As the prologue begins to unfold the historic manifestation of the light in the incarnation of the Word, John the Baptist is introduced as a primary witness to that light (1:6–8, 15).

The light that came into the world is described as 'true' (1:9), suggesting a contrast, 'not simply with what is false but with what is earlier and provisional or anticipatory in the history of God's gracious self-disclosure'.[32] Most likely, a comparison is being made with law and wisdom as the source of divine light (cf. Ps. 119:105; Prov. 6:23). Describing the true light as shining upon everyone, John highlights 'the universal scope of Jesus' coming and the potential spiritual enlightenment available to all who believe'.[33]

When the true light came into the world, 'the world did not know him' (1:10). More narrowly, when he came to his own property or place (1:11, *ta idia*; cf. 16:32; 19:27), his own people (*hoi idioi*) did not receive him. Here the focus narrows to the covenant people of God (cf. Exod. 19:5, 'my treasured possession among all peoples'). John goes on to document how the nation as a whole did not recognize or receive the Son of God, but a believing community emerged from the midst of Israel, whom Jesus called 'his own' (13:1, *tous idious*).[34]

---

32. Carson, *John*, p. 122. Compare the use of the same adjective (*alēthinon*, 'true') in 4:23; 6:32; 15:1.

33. Köstenberger, *John*, p. 36. External illumination in the sense of objective revelation is meant by the claim that Jesus is the light of the world (cf. 8:12). Such revelation requires a believing response to become internal illumination.

34. Carson, *John*, pp. 125–126, establishes that receiving Jesus in John's Gospel means entrusting oneself to him, acknowledging his claims and confessing him.

Using another term applicable to national Israel, John affirms that only those who 'believed in his name' (cf. 2:23; 3:18; 20:31) were given the authority to become 'children of God' (1:12; cf. Exod. 4:22–23; Deut. 14:1; 1 John 3:1–2).[35] The Father's role in the process is clarified with the expression 'born of God', which anticipates what is said in 3:1–7 about the need for regeneration by his Spirit.

The Word and God's glory

The eternal Word became flesh and took up residence with his people in a more personal and intimate way than under the Old Covenant (1:14).[36] In due course John reveals that the incarnate Word was Jesus Christ (1:17). With the expression 'we have seen his glory' the author claims to have been among those who witnessed the glory of God in the person and work of Christ. That glory was first manifested through his 'signs' (2:11; 11:4, 40), but Jesus was supremely glorified in his death and exaltation (7:39; 12:16, 23; 13:31–32). The glory is further defined as 'glory as of the only Son from the Father', introducing a more intimate way of describing the relationship between God and the Word.[37]

'Full of grace and truth' (1:14) recalls the way God is described in Exodus 34:6, when he revealed his glory to Moses (cf. Exod. 33:18–19). God's lovingkindness and faithfulness describe his covenant commitment to his people, which found ultimate expression in the sending of his Son. This terminology suggests covenant renewal or fulfilment for Israel with the incarnation of the Word.

35. Köstenberger, *John*, p. 38, suggests that the phrase 'in his name' may place particular emphasis on the fact that 'in order to believe in Jesus, one must believe that he bears the divine name'.

36. The expression *eskēnōsen en hēmin* literally means 'pitched his tent among them', recalling the significance of the tabernacle as a sign of God's glorious presence in the midst of Israel. Cf. Peterson, *Engaging with God*, pp. 32–36, 43–45, 93–95.

37. Köstenberger, *John*, p. 42–44, argues that the expression *monogenous para patros* in 1:14 means that Jesus is the Father's 'one-of-a-kind Son'.

With the expression 'from his fullness we have all received, grace upon grace' (1:16) John expands on the final claim in 1:14. All who believed in the incarnate Son received grace beyond any grace previously experienced.[38]

If 1:17 is read as an explanation of 1:16, John is not opposing law and grace. In effect he says grace came through the law, but this was followed by the ultimate expression of God's grace in Jesus Christ. Indeed,

> the law that was *given* through Moses, and the grace and truth that *came* through Jesus Christ (v. 17), alike sprang from the fullness of the Word (v. 16), whether in his pre-existent oneness with the Father, or in his status as the Word-made-flesh. It is from that 'fullness' that we have received 'one grace replacing another'.[39]

John concludes his prologue by saying, 'No one has ever seen God; the only God, who is at the Father's side, he has made him known' (1:18; cf. 5:37; 6:46; 14:9). Not even Moses saw God's 'face' (Exod. 33:20), though he witnessed God's glory and experienced an amazing revelation of his character and will (Exod. 33:21 – 34:10). However, the unique relationship between Father and Son made it possible for Jesus to 'overcome the vast gulf that had existed between God and humankind up to that point – despite the law'.[40]

---

38. Wallace, *Greek Grammar*, pp. 364–368, observes that the Greek preposition *anti* can mean 'in place of' and can be used in the sense of substitution or succession. Carson, *John*, pp. 131–132, suggests that *charin anti charitos* means 'grace instead of grace', and says this is explained in 1:17 (so also Köstenberger, *John*, pp. 46–47).

39. Carson, *John*, p. 134 (original emphasis). Carson, pp. 131–134, helpfully reviews a variety of positions that have been taken on law and grace in the Fourth Gospel. Cf. W. J. Dumbrell, 'Law and Grace: The Nature of the Contrast in John 1:17', *EvQ* 47 (1986), pp. 25–37.

40. Köstenberger, *John*, p. 48.

Knowing the Father and the Son

Failing to know God

The prologue claims that when the true light came into the world, 'the world did not know him' (1:9–10; cf. 17:25). At one level the Gospel presents this as a problem of *understanding*. When Jesus began to teach and manifest his glory in signs, his disciples believed in him (2:11), but Jesus knew that he could not trust the crowds to understand and respond appropriately (2:23–25; cf. 6:64). Nicodemus represents this wider group when he confesses, 'we know that you are a teacher come from God' (3:2), but does not understand what Jesus is saying when he speaks of the need to be 'born of the Spirit' (3:7–10; cf. 10:6).

When Jesus declares himself to be 'the bread that came down from heaven', the Jewish leaders acknowledge him as the son of earthly parents only and cannot understand his claim to have come from God (6:41–42; cf. 7:26–29). When he describes himself as 'the light of the world' (8:12), the Pharisees question the validity of his testimony and cannot understand that he speaks to them as the agent of the Father (8:13–27). Nevertheless, Jesus predicts that when they have 'lifted' him 'up' they will know his true identity and authority (8:28).[41]

The Jewish leaders do not truly know the one they confess as their God, but Jesus claims to know him and to have come in order to do his will (8:54–55; cf. 4:34). They know that God spoke to Moses, but they do not know where Jesus came from (9:29). Even the disciples do not understand certain things until Jesus is glorified (2:22; 4:31–34; 12:16; 13:7, 28).

But failure to know the Father and the Son is also identified with *unresponsiveness*. As in the Old Testament, to receive the Word of

---

41. Carson, *John*, p. 345, observes that 'by this John is not saying that all of Jesus' opponents will be converted in the wake of the cross. But if they do come to know who Jesus is, they will know it most surely because of the cross.'

God implies 'something more than mere intellectual apprehension'.[42] Jesus knows that his opponents do not receive him because they do not have the love of God within them (5:42). He exposes the link between wanting to do God's will and knowing whether his teaching is from God (7:17). People do not understand him because they cannot bear to hear his word (8:43). Those who claim to be Abraham's children show that they do not know God, because they are not prepared to do his will and seek to get rid of Jesus (8:39–55). Stubbornness, hardness of heart and spiritual blindness are revealed in the way many respond to Jesus and his mighty works (e.g. 9:13–33; 12:36–43).

The knowledge that saves

Positively, John uses the verb 'know' to describe the sort of relationship with God made possible by believing Jesus' words. At a climactic point in the narrative, when many disciples had turned back and no longer walked with him, Peter acknowledges that Jesus has the words of eternal life and confesses, 'we have believed, and have come to know, that you are the Holy One of God' (6:69; cf. 4:42).

Claiming to be 'the good shepherd', Jesus describes the relationship he has with his 'sheep' in terms of mutual knowledge: 'I know my own and my own know me' (10:14; cf. 10:27). This is compared with the relationship the Son has with the Father: 'just as the Father knows me and I know the Father; and I lay down my life for the sheep' (10:15).[43] It is a relationship that involves self-sacrificing love on his part, and demands that disciples show the same love for one another (13:1–17). Jesus indicates that those who have known him

---

42. Dodd, *Interpretation*, p. 157. Dodd, p. 156, observes that 'the world did not know him' (1:10) is followed by 'his own people did not receive him' (1:11), where 'the second clause at least suggests that the will and not only the intelligence is at fault'. Cf. Isa. 1:3; Jer. 9:3, 6.

43. Dodd, ibid., pp. 166–168, points out that the knowledge the Son has of the Father is associated with his divine commission and with his obedience to the divine word (7:28–29; 8:54–55). But the knowledge he imparts is also a 'vision' of the Father (12:45; 14:9).

have known the Father, because he is 'in the Father' and the Father is in him (14:7–11).

In the Fourth Gospel, as in the Old Testament, 'man's knowledge of God is correlative with, and dependent on, God's "knowledge" of man'.[44] God knows those who are his (10:14), he chooses them (13:18; 15:16) and brings them to himself (6:44; 12:32). This knowledge is associated with his grace and election, and expresses the establishment of a covenantal relationship with them. But the critical difference under the New Covenant is that God does this through the agency of his Son, who is the Word made flesh.

The Holy Spirit also has a significant role to play. Jesus teaches that the world cannot receive the Spirit of truth 'because it neither sees him nor knows him', but the disciples are assured that they know him, 'for he dwells with you and will be in you' (14:17). Jesus speaks about the day when he will come to them and they will know that 'I am in my Father, and you in me, and I in you' (14:20). Most commentators take this as a reference to his resurrection, though it possibly refers to his coming through the Spirit at Pentecost.[45] Jesus predicts that the Spirit will bear witness to him as the truth and lead his disciples 'into all the truth' (14:17; 15:26; 16:13). Since Jesus is 'the truth' (14:6), knowledge of the truth is relational and not simply intellectual.

John the Baptist had pointed to Jesus as 'the Lamb of God, who takes away the sin of the world' (1:29, 36). Jesus spoke about his approaching sacrifice in terms of his flesh and blood given 'for the life of the world' (6:51–58; cf. 3:14–17). He also identified himself as the good shepherd who lays down his life for the sheep (10:15, 17–18). Dedicating himself to do the Father's will and going to the cross for the salvation of his people, Jesus declares that 'this is eternal life, that they know you the only true God, and Jesus Christ whom you have sent' (17:3). To know God truly is to live before him in an

---

44. Ibid., pp. 160–161. Cf. Ps. 139; Jer. 1:5; 12:3; Hos. 5:3; Amos 3:2.

45. Carson, *John*, pp. 501–502, sides with the majority, but Köstenberger, *John*, p. 439, argues that Jesus' coming to his followers 'in the Spirit' is the more plausible view.

eternal relationship (cf. Hos. 6:1–3). His self-consecration in death is clearly an essential step in the securing of that relationship (17:19).

Being taught by God

John proclaims the fulfilment of Jeremiah's promise that 'they shall all know me, from the least of them to the greatest' (Jer. 31:34) by showing that, through the incarnation of the Word, consummated in his death, 'knowledge and vision of God were brought to men as never before'.[46] Critical to this knowledge is the teaching Jesus brings from the Father, assuring his disciples that he came from the Father and was sent by him (17:7–8, 25). Indeed, Jesus assures everyone who continues in his word that they will know the truth, 'and the truth will set you free' (8:31–32). True believers absorb his teaching and live by it. Those who hear him and do not believe show that they are not from God and that God is not their Father (8:41–47; cf. 3:21; 18:37).

When 'the Jews' raise objections about his claim to be 'the bread that came down from heaven', Jesus declares, 'No one can come to me unless the Father who sent me draws him. And I will raise him up on the last day' (6:41–44). The Father must draw people to the Son, who is the agent of eschatological salvation through his death and resurrection. Indeed, Jesus declares that 'All that the Father gives me will come to me, and whoever comes to me I will never cast out' (6:37). Those who refuse to come to him show that they are unwilling to learn from God, since 'everyone who has heard and learned from the Father comes to me' (6:45).

In making this claim, Jesus paraphrases Isaiah 54:13, 'And they will all be taught by God' (6:45).[47] This is similar to Jeremiah's prediction

---

46. Dodd, *Interpretation*, p. 165. Dodd, p. 169, concludes that the vision is of the true nature of God 'in the unity of Father and Son'. But 'the content of knowledge is enlarged to include the unity of men in and with Christ, in God' (14:20).

47. Carson, *John*, p. 293, points out that Isa. 54:13 is applied typologically: 'the messianic community and the dawning of the saving reign of God are the typological fulfilment of the restoration of Jerusalem after the Babylonian exile'.

that 'they shall all know me, from the least of them to the greatest' (Jer. 31:34), Ezekiel's promise of a new heart and a new spirit (Ezek. 36:24–26), and Joel's expectation of the Spirit's transforming work in the last days (Joel 2:28–32). The introductory words in John 6:45 'it is written in the Prophets' could indicate that this is a general theme in the prophetic writings, though some take it to refer to 'the Prophets' as the particular section of the Scriptures from which the quote is derived. The Father draws people to the Son by teaching them and convincing them about his claims.[48] But Jesus strangely uses a promise that *all* of God's people will be taught by him as a challenge to those within Israel who refuse to come to him!

The 'all' in the quotation from Isaiah 54:13 is qualified by the immediate claim that no one has seen the Father 'except he who is from God; he has seen the Father' (6:46). In other words, the teaching about the true nature of God and his salvation is mediated through the Son. People need to *hear* and *learn* from the one who has *seen* the Father. No one else can convey such revelation (1:17–18; 3:13; 5:37), and it is not obtained by personal, mystical experiences. Those who receive the teaching brought by the Son and 'believe in his name' show themselves to be the true children of God (1:12–13; 6:47).

So there is a process of election at work within Israel, as the Son of God comes to 'his own' and reveals the character and will of the Father. In John 6 we are informed about a 'cooperative effort between the Father and the Son in bringing a person to salvation'.[49] Along with this predestinarian emphasis the passage insists that those who hear the voice of the Son of God must come and believe (6:35–40, 47–48; cf. 10:27–30), but can do so only by the Father's enabling (6:44; cf. 3:3–8).

---

48. In John 14:26–27, 16:12–15 Jesus makes it clear that the Spirit will have this teaching role. This parallels the emphasis in 1 John 2:20, 26–27 about the anointing of the Spirit, which 'teaches you about everything'.

49. Köstenberger, *John*, p. 214. Note that the glorified Son will draw 'all people' to himself (12:32) but, as in 6:45, 'all' does not mean everyone without exception. The context suggests a reference to believers from all nations (cf. 12:20–23). So the meaning is 'all people without distinction'.

Conclusion

The allusion to the promised New Covenant in 1 John 2:20, 27 takes us to the heart of the letter's concern. Interpreted in the light of Ezekiel 11:19–20, 36:26–27, Jeremiah's prophecy is used as part of an appeal to continue in the knowledge of God and to experience its ongoing effect. This knowledge of the Father and the Son comes from the apostolic witnesses and is confirmed in believers by the indwelling Spirit of God. When the full impact of Jeremiah's prophecy on the argument of 1 John is uncovered, links with the Gospel suggest that the fulfilment of its predictions is proclaimed in various ways there too.

For example, in both the Epistle and the Gospel 'eternal life' is a particular way of describing the relationship with God made possible through the incarnation, death and resurrection of Jesus and the gift of the Holy Spirit. This means a new quality of life in the present, with the certainty of enjoying God's presence for ever. Such a relationship with God encourages righteous and loving behaviour in those who are genuine believers. In other words, the Johannine literature proclaims a transformed lifestyle arising from a new knowledge or experience of God in Jesus Christ.

Christians no longer need mediating teachers or prophets to convey the knowledge of God. Jesus is the definitive source of that knowledge because of his unique relationship to the Father as Son. What he reveals about the Father and his saving purpose was first conveyed to the world through the apostles, guided and taught by the Holy Spirit. The same Spirit keeps believers in the truth, as they resist false teaching and remain faithful to the apostolic testimony. Although John does not explicitly say so, the Spirit will work in and through believers, as they remind each other of apostolic teaching and apply it to their everyday lives.[50]

---

50. Since John reveals that the Spirit works through the testimony of believers to convict the world of sin, righteousness and judgment (John 16:8–11), it is reasonable to argue that he viewed the Spirit as also having a ministry to believers through their engagement with one another.

The death of Jesus is presented in the Fourth Gospel as the means by which the sin of the world is taken away and eternal life is made available for all who believe and come to him (1:29, 36; 3:14–16; 6:53–58). Put another way, it is the means by which the good shepherd rescues his sheep for eternity (10:14–18). In 1 John the focus is on the forgiveness and purification from sins continually made available by Jesus as heavenly intercessor, on the basis of his once-for-all sacrifice (1:7–9; 2:1–2; 4:10). In effect, this teaching, which is particularly linked with God's faithfulness and justice, proclaims the fulfilment of Jeremiah's promise concerning the ongoing provision for sin under the New Covenant.

Knowing the love of God in sending his Son to deal with the problem of sin and make eternal life possible is the motivation for love and keeping God's commandments. The transformation of believers envisaged in the Johannine literature is the result of the Spirit's regenerative work and the impact of the gospel on their heart (John 3:3–8; 7:37–39; 1 John 2:29 – 3:10; 4:13; 5:1). Here again there is an echo of Jeremiah's prediction about the change of attitude and behaviour that the New Covenant will bring.

John's Gospel deals much more obviously with the salvation-historical implications of the coming of the Son of God than John's letters do. Covenant renewal for Israel is implied in various ways, but a process of election takes place *within* Israel, as Jesus teaches and offers signs of his identity and saving work. A new community forms around Jesus, who is 'the true vine' (John 15:1–11; cf. Isa. 5:1–7). The ultimate expression of God's grace in Jesus Christ is salvation for people from every nation, not simply for renewed Israelites (John 3:16; 12:32). This implies the fulfilment of the promise about the blessing of the nations through the offspring of Abraham (Gen. 12:3).

There is a particular interest in the Fourth Gospel in why Jesus' own people do not know him and will not receive him. Associated with this is a developing picture of how God knows, chooses and brings to himself the people of the New Covenant. As in 1 John, the transforming work of God takes place through the knowledge imparted by the Son and applied by the Spirit to the heart of believers. This knowledge is not merely intellectual, but involves the establishment of an eternal relationship with God as Trinity.

Pastorally, the Johannine writings remind us of the foundational importance of knowing the Father through the mediation of the Son and the work of the Holy Spirit. Even as the author points to Jesus as the ultimate revelation of God's character and will, so must contemporary evangelists. Christ-centred evangelism brings people into a *new relationship* with God. Moreover, as the author highlights the need for Jesus' death and resurrection to secure an eternal relationship with God, so also must contemporary evangelists. The gospel is about *reconciliation* with God through the person and work of the Son. Evangelism with these twin emphases will bring people to experience what the prophecy of the New Covenant predicted.

Believers need to be taught about the regenerative work of the Spirit and be told about the Spirit's ability to keep them in the truth. Gospel preaching should be accompanied by prayer for the Spirit to work in the hearts of those addressed. When belief and commitment to Christ result, these can be identified as signs of the Spirit's presence and of God's electing grace. Ministry to one another by the Spirit's enabling should be seen as a further sign of God's covenant love and faithfulness to his people.

However, challenged about the destructive and divisive effect of false teaching, believers should be encouraged to test what is presented to them, evaluating everything by the apostolic teaching and the Spirit's confirming testimony. The tragedy of denial and betrayal presented in both the Gospel and the Epistle sounds a warning across the centuries, even to those who count themselves the beneficiaries of the New Covenant.

Assured of God's desire to transform us from within, and ultimately conform us to the likeness of his Son, we can be exhorted to purify ourselves, 'as he is pure' (1 John 3:3). Following John's example, exhortations to godly living should be based on a clear exposition of what the Father has provided for his children through

the Son and the Spirit. God does not ask us to live in obedience to
him without giving us the resources to make this possible. In the
glorious riches of the New Covenant, God offers us all that we need
to be faithful and fruitful disciples, until we 'see him as he is' (3:2).

INDEX OF SCRIPTURE REFERENCES